# Love, GOD

Real experiences with God, Jesus,
The Virgin Mary and The Holy Spirit

ELIZABETH COOK

**BALBOA.**
PRESS
A DIVISION OF HAY HOUSE

Balboa Press books may be ordered through booksellers or by contacting:

Balboa Press
A Division of Hay House
1663 Liberty Drive
Bloomington, IN 47403
www.balboapress.com
1-(877) 407-4847

ISBN: 978-1-4525-4095-5 (sc)
ISBN: 978-1-4525-4097-9 (hc)
ISBN: 978-1-4525-4096-2 (e)

Library of Congress Control Number: 2011919436

Printed in the United States of America

Balboa Press rev. date: 11/17/2011

# Acknowledgements:

God

Spirit

My husband Kevin and our children Alexis and Adam
and our baby In Spirit, Jesse

Laurie Stimpson

Mackenzie Phillips

Chris and Tim Murphy

Barbara Fluck

Flea for his inspiring quote I keep by my computer

I NEVER THOUGHT THAT THE path of my life would lead me to writing a book for God. Yep, I said FOR God. It wasn't till maybe 6 years ago when I saw a nice little old psychic lady that my life's purpose showed itself. She asked me what I wanted to do. That was a simple question. "I just want to help people." Pretty simple answer but it was very surprising to me. I had never thought about anything past being a mom at that time. What kind of "help" I meant was not like the medical kind like going to work in a hospital. I'm not good with cuts and stuff. What I thought it meant was that I would be on a path that would lead me to being a psychic medium. But today, as I have realized in the last year, my purpose goes in a different form of helping others. Just like in the book, The Legend of the Three Trees, "Sometimes, the dreams that we have for ourselves are much smaller than the dreams that God has for us. The three trees' dreams came true, just not in the way they imagined. And so it is with each of us. For if we follow God's path, we will travel far beyond even our greatest dreams." I read that book to my kids and I cry every time because I see the truth in those words. So I am going to go with what I know in my heart, what pulls at me; what I pray for. To help people in the way that God wants me to and write about our stories together. This book is a journal of experiences I have written since May of 2010. Amazingly, I had no computer to write it all on but within a week of asking God if I should do this, one of our friends just GAVE us one . . . he didn't need it anymore!! It was meant to be. Some of my experiences happened before 2010 but most of them have happened since. I keep writing and they keep happening. It's pretty amazing. It's not only just about God but also The Virgin Mary, Jesus, The Holy

Spirit and a lot of other subjects we can gain wisdom from. All of these personal experiences are The Truth.

I hope that whoever reads this will find peace in knowing that God really IS involved in our daily life and that He loves each and every one of us. I feel that these are important things God would like you to know. May it inspire you to connect with Him. Thank you.

God's Blessings,

Elizabeth

Psalm 37:3

*-Trust in the Lord and Do Good*

# MY LITERAL SIGN

Yes, I went to church when I was a little girl. I had my First Communion but after that we stopped going. My mom raised us Catholic up until my brother and I put up a stink about not going to church because, "dad didn't have to!" I never really gave it much thought until my divorce. I had always told myself I would know when it was time to leave my marriage. I would just know. I had left a few times and taken the kids with me for a night or weekend but always would come back home. Then one day I thought to myself, "if I die tomorrow I'll be dying unhappy." So that night I sat in front of my then husband and didn't plan on saying anything but my soul spoke, no flowed, pouring out of my mouth were the words, "I can't take this anymore." And he understood. To say our marriage wasn't good would be an understatement. I never was honest with my friends and family about what really went on behind closed doors. To give a person wise advice to leave is being a good friend but they need to be able to come to that conclusion on their own. I stayed all those years because I honestly thought that I could help him but I now realize that the only person that can help you is yourself. I think he liked the "idea" of having a family much more than actually having one. SO. He left. And I raised the kids on my own. Then about a month after he had left (he had moved 4hrs away) I found out some terrible lies he had told about me to a new girlfriend. Which crushed me. And I cried and cried and cried. My daughter, then 4, would come give me hugs while I layed in bed crying and tell me it was all going to be ok. SHE was comforting ME! So one day we were driving in the country to my aunt's house and I took a road I didn't travel much and there was a sign on a mailbox that read, "GOD SHALL WIPE AWAY YOUR TEARS"-

1

Revelation 21:4. And he did. The very next day. I woke up and the tears were gone, the sobbing gone and I started my new life. And you know, I had honestly forgotten about God up until that sign. I didn't have a relationship with him then. But he was there for me when I needed him. I didn't realize that this was just the beginning of things to come.

# THE VIRGIN MARY

SHE CAME TO MY NEW husband, Kevin and I when we were still dating in the living room of my old house in Green Bay. This had been a 3 tall tapered candle/flower arrangement that I had gotten from a radio station designer purse giveaway where my friend won the grand prize. I asked for the flowers because they were pretty. All had been given away as door prizes except this one. It had burned about halfway down that night and then it wasn't lit again till Kevin came to visit me. All the wax burnt off but remaining was what looks like Mary. The flames were blue and green and really neat. I didn't even notice what was happening till it was at this point so Kevin, being the strict Catholic boy he is, was very calm when I said, "that looks like the Virgin Mary!" and he goes, "yeah, I've been watching it". So I got out my camera and started taking pictures. Then I was going to blow it out cause really, if someone can sell a grilled cheese on Ebay that has her image I could sell this, right!? Oh no! I was on my knees and took a big inhale to blow out the candles and that flower in the middle BURST into flames! So I just let it burn down to nothing. I got the hint! The flowers make her crown above her head and she is praying over what I interpret as the Trinity.

# TO EVERYONE THAT PRAYS FOR GOD TO SEND THEM SOMEONE

THE FIRST MEMORY OF GOING to church besides when I was little and the midnight masses for Christmas with the family was when I was about 20. I went to Christmas Day mass with my grandma and I prayed for God to, "send me a man". HAHA. Yep. I did. And He did. A couple days later a guy I had met called me up and took me out on a date. We saw Titanic. Then we hung out the night before New Year's Eve at his grandparents cabin out in the woods with my friend, Nikki and his friends. I gotta tell you the funny part of that night though. I passed out on a plate of venison. Nasty. This after saying, "Nikki says I'm a princess and I can have a puppy." So MY friend met one of HIS friends and they started dating after that night. My guy ended up having a girlfriend already so he was a loser. This I found out about a month later. BUT here is the thing. When God answers your prayers, if it's meant to be, it could be totally different but WAY BETTER. I ended up being the 3rd wheel with my friend and his friend and when they broke up I ended up being just one of the guys in their group of brothers, cousins and friends. I had needed a pseudo family. My parents had divorced and I wasn't getting along with my brother at the time or my parents for that matter. The Jahnke Boys were my new family and we spent a lot of time together. They lived on a farm and we'd watch movies in the movie room or have fires out at what they called, "Dodge" or they'd come over to my house after flag football and hang out. It was what I needed. They are all great guys! And those memories are some of the closest to my heart. So even though I had prayed for God to send me a man, He did. 8 of them! :) And I often think that that was just part of God's plan for me later in life (about 9 years later) when I met my now husband, Kevin. He has many of the same qualities of the Jahnke Boys that I love so much.

# DIVINE INTERVENTION

THE FIRST SUMMER I LIVED alone with my 2 kids it was super hot out. I lived on one of the busiest streets in Green Bay—in the downtown area where all the old houses are really neat but it's borderline ghetto. Not a place I let my kids play outside on their own. The house across the street was always having the cops there. I had a really nice lady that lived next to me so I felt relatively safe. I would always open up the front and back doors when I came home from work and left the windows open all day. Then one night I caught the nightly news and it said that to keep your house cool if you don't have AC you should leave everything shut and pull the shades. So I did that the next day. I'd give it a try and when we got home it WAS a lot cooler! So I left everything closed up.

I was doing the dishes in the kitchen and the kids were upstairs when I heard this loud rattling noise coming from the front door. The handle being shaken violently. And then the door bell ringing. Luckily the kids didn't hear it and come downstairs because I peeked around the corner and saw a man peering in the window that I had never seen before and then walk away to the house across the street. The drug house. Luckily the kids had not heard him and came down. I hid. Then grabbed my phone. About 3 minutes later 2 girls pulled into my driveway so I took my phone out with me and asked if I could help them. They said they were looking for D. I said, "there is no one by that name living here." and then they replied, "we are supposed to pick him up here." Then they repeated my address. And said, "there are 2 kids here". Which shocked me. Had he planned on robbing me and taking my kids? Who knows what! I'll never know, and maybe you could say that I'm jumping to conclusions but when he told them there are 2 kids something really bad must have been planned. And it was avoided. The news from the night before had been a warning and I listened. THANK GOD

# THE FIRST TIME JESUS KNOCKED

I HAD FINALLY GOTTEN A cross for my house. I got a simple wooden one and hung it up in my living room. Before this my aunt had given me a painting that she had given my grandparents of Jesus knocking on a door. They had always hung it in their bedroom. So it was up in mine. I got the wooden cross because somehow it seemed like one my grandfather would've liked. The first night I had it up I was sitting in my living room watching tv. The kids were upstairs sleeping. I heard 3 loud knocks. I couldn't tell if it was the front door or the backdoor. Like it was from every part of the the downstairs. I quick turned on both porch lights and didn't see a thing. Then got a little frightened (living on my own and all) and hit the deck. Then jokingly I said, "if that's you Jesus you can come in!!"

# GOD UNDERSTANDS

MY HOUSE IN GREEN BAY was on the market for sale for over 3 years. In the meantime I had had my divorce finalized and met Kevin and had planned on moving to Minnesota with my kids to start a new life with him there. So our lives were pretty much on hold till the house sold. This was upsetting. So one night I fell asleep after crying to God about why can't we just move there? Why is it taking so long for the house to sell? I've been patient and it's hard to keep believing a buyer will come. And yes, I said the 9 Hail Mary's, 9 Glory B's and 9 Our Father's for 9 days. Heck, I did them for like a month. I buried the St. Joseph statue upside down in the yard. The kids and I prayed every November to Christmas the St. Andrew advent prayer for it to sell. Nothing was working. And so i was crying and fell asleep. I sleep with a rosary under my pillow. I went through a phase of saying it for a couple months straight when I learned it but then stopped and just took to having it with me when I slept. I read daily readings from a magazine called <u>The Upper Room</u>. It's really good actually. So here I fell asleep crying to God and as I woke up the next morning I remember reading in my dream the title in big bold black lettering the daily reading for the day just like it would look like in the magazine. It read **I UNDERSTAND** and then my hand grazed my rosary which woke me up. And I felt better. But better isn't really the word for it. Comforted. Yeah. Comforted.

# SEALED WITH THE GIFT OF THE HOLY SPIRIT

WHEN I FIRST MET KEVIN he said something about the Eucharist and I didn't know what that was. He thought I was joking. Nope. So when we started dating I was open to going to church with him. Even though I thought that you don't have to go to church to believe in God. I probably never would have gone again if Father hadn't said something about all of us having gifts from God. I had felt like an outsider and that made me feel better. The year after Kevin and I started dating I took Confirmation classes with a friend. I liked going to church. On my 30th birthday I was confirmed. And after I was anointed with the oils I took my seat next to another girl. Then my head got all hot and started to tingle where the oil was on my forehead. I turned to her and asked her if her's felt like that also. She looked at me like I was Crazy! But I truly believe that I really was sealed with the gift of the Holy Spirit that day.

# FOOTPRINTS ON MY BACK

I HAVE A REALLY LONG Footprints poster hanging in my bedroom.

Footprints

One night a man had a dream. He dreamed he was walking along the beach with the Lord. Across the sky flashed scenes from his life. For each scene, he noticed two sets of footprints in the sand: one belonging to him, and the other to the Lord.

When the last scene of his life flashed before him, he looked back at the footprints in the sand. He noticed that many times along the path of his life there was only one set of footprints. He also noticed that it happened at the very lowest and saddest times in his life.

This really bothered him and he questioned the Lord about it, "Lord, you said that once I decided to follow you, you'd walk with me all the way. But I have noticed that during the most troublesome times in my life, there is only one set of footprints. I don't understand why when I needed you most you would leave me."

The Lord replied, "My child, My precious child, I love you and I would never leave you. During your times of trial and suffering, when you see only one set of footprints, it was then that I carried you."

-Author Unknown

This was a gift from my dad for my first apartment when I was 21. I used to keep it in the bathroom, you know, beach theme . . . . One morning in the winter of '06 I was getting dressed to go up to my grandma's house for Sunday lunch with her and my kids. It was our weekly thing to go eat with Granner. That morning as I walked past the Footprints poster it flew out and grazed my back. I didn't have a shirt on and it made me jump forward and reach for where it grazed me. I thought that was odd. So I walked past it again to see if it was just a fluke. Nope. I walked past even faster and still nothing. So I said, "ok God, what is going to happen today?" This was my heads up. So we ate with Granner and instead of leaving at 2 or 3 in the afternoon, like we usually did, we ended up visiting until it was dark and past the kids bedtime. She lived 30 minutes north of us. We NEVER stayed until dark. So on the way home going 70 mph with my 2 children asleep in the backseat with the roads just perfectly clear and we hadn't had snow for a few days I hit a patch of black ice. Which seemed to last forever. And I wanted to freak out but just repeated, "whoa, whoa, whoa" and kept the wheel even. No sudden movements. I am amazed at how calm I was. And we got over it safely. Why? Because God or angels, whoever it was, CARRIED US. Just like it says in the Footprints poem.

# THE FOOTPRINTS POSTER
# MOVED AGAIN!

THIS TIME IT WAS OCTOBER of '08. I woke up in my bedroom at around 1am to a noise I couldn't place. So I thought about the noise and realized it was the poster. It had fallen off the wall. So I said, "what is going to happen today God?" Healing. Strength. Letting go. You see, it had been a few months since the kids dad had last seen them. It was like pulling teeth to get him to take them. Always a last minute the day of excuse. Which led to me having two crying kids in my backseat later in the day when I picked them up from daycare cause they had wanted to go. It killed me. My heart broke for them. We always packed their bags the night before so we could leave from daycare and drive to Stevens Point. Sometimes I'd even drive back on Sunday to get them myself for him to see them. I was doing my best to keep the connection of them to their dad. So whenever the last minute bail out would happen I would have to leave my desk at work and go out and sit in my car and cry for them. Why didn't he want them? Why wouldn't he call them? Why wouldn't he even come visit them for a day if he didn't want them to stay overnight? How could he come back to Green Bay to party with his friends and not even stop to see them? Sigh. The list could go on. But THIS DAY when the crappy excuse came I didn't go out to my car. I was inspired by God to write my ex a letter. I told him we would be moving to Minnesota in a month. This was his out. Which i knew he would take. I told him that when he is ready to be a father to the kids he is more than welcome to come back into their lives but I am not going to MAKE him see them anymore. I wouldn't set up the weekends-which were supposed to be every other. I wouldn't say another word unless he asked me to see them. He had to take the initiative. He hasn't seen them in almost 3 years. He doesn't call to check on them even. Nothing. I have called and talked to him and told him the door is open whenever he wants. Even offered for him to come and stay with us at our home for a weekend! I even sent him a book by Dr. Wayne Dyer called <u>Excuses Begone</u> for Christmas last year. Obviously I pray for him. Even when I was in confession telling Father how it's hard to not hate him and at that same time he is sending a text lying about why he isn't sending child support, I pray for him. Writing him that letter was freeing. Again, God carried me. This time to take a higher road. He made me realize you can't make someone be a dad. And that night I read a random page from the Bible. Psalm 36:1-5 . . . ." Empty and false are the words of their mouth;they have ceased to be wise and do good. In their beds they hatch plots" God knows all. Sees all. He knows what is going on and He works with it and turns it into something good. The kids have a wonderful step dad in Kevin. He has rescued them and will always be their hero. They have a positive male role model in him. And he loves them as his own and they love him. You can see it on their faces. He is their Dad/Daddy. He can't take their biological fathers spot but he can sure make his own.

# WHAT IF JESUS LIVED PAST
# THE CRUCIFIXION?

WHAT IF HE DIED ON the cross but 3 days later when it says that he rose, he actually came back to life TO LIVE LIFE? What if he did??? Then shouldn't we all be happy for him?? If he DID, then that means he was able to live to be an old man, have a family, be in love, and live a happy life! There are different ways to interpret the Bible of what happened after the crucifixion. Read it for yourselves and keep an open mind to the possibility . . . . I had never thought about that before reading a book by Sylvia Browne called The Two Marys about 3 months ago. Now I don't agree with everything Sylvia says BUT I will say that after reading her book the way that it shook me and I couldn't stop crying for like a week and thinking about it constantly even when I was running each night, she's on to something. I think he lived. The picture of Jesus praying in the Garden of Gethsemane has always been my favorite. I have always been pulled to it. Maybe because I can relate to praying really hard with all my heart . . . . and if God answers our prayers than why not answer his own son's?? Jesus was prepared to die and went through with it but I think God gave him a second chance at living life. It IS possible. After all, He WANTED to live. I told my daughter, who is 9 about this. She went to religion class and told the teacher Jesus lived and she was told, "that is a BIG SIN LIE". Strict Catholics. Something has always bothered me about a picture I took of Jesus on Easter Sunday about 3 years ago. Of all the places on the highway to pull over and take that picture it has a sign that reads WRONG WAY in it. I've always been upset that I didn't realize it then and move so it wouldn't be in the way but the colors in the sky were fading and I had to take the picture fast. You see, I had been explaining to the kids that Easter Sunday is the day that Jesus rose from the dead. The sun in my rear view mirror was so orange and bright it hurt to look at it-this was at sunset by the way. Then as I was telling them about Jesus I looked out my passenger side window and what had been 2 very distinct lines of pink and purple running horizontally had the pink now shooting straight up through the purple. I had never seen anything like it before and instinctively pointed to it and said, "There's Jesus!" When I found a safe place to pull over it had faded drastically but you could still see it. I only wish I had gotten a picture of it immediately. Anyways, Wrong Way could be interpreted as the wrong way he died. Now I feel like that sign was on purpose. It makes sense now. He rose from the dead BUT went on to live. He did not ascend to Heaven at that time. Two weeks after reading Sylvia's book I had to contact my dad for a school assignment that my daughter was doing. A family crest. I knew we were Irish but needed more than that. He texts me back we are Swiss too. And he thinks we are a descendant of one of the Knights Templar. If I hadn't read that book I would have had no clue what he was talking about and blown it off. My dad is SO not religious. He didn't even want to take my grandma to Easter mass this year so as not to go into a church. So that statement surprised the hell out of me. Seems there was a Koch I guess and that is how our name Cook was originally spelled. NOW it all makes sense. IF we are than all this that has happened to me makes a lot of sense and I'm on the right path. No wonder Jesus surviving the crucifixion hit me like a ton of bricks! No wonder all these things that happen to me that sound not even possible have happened. Now I feel weird at church. On top of feeling weird when I don't believe that the Eucharist is really the body of Jesus (I believe it is just a way to remember him-not really him), I feel like my views are completely different from the other people around me. I'd love to open communication with them about all these things but maybe they are just not ready to see or hear it yet.

Today, April 20, 2011

This morning on the Christian radio station I heard them say that Psalm 22 is related to the accounts of Jesus' Passion. So I read it. Amazing. I have The New American Bible-the Saint Joseph addition. I would like anyone reading this to get your own Bible and read Psalm 22 all the way through. Verses 31,32 "And I will live for the Lord; my descendants will serve you. The generation to come will be told of the Lord, that they may proclaim to a people yet unborn the deliverance you have brought." Why aren't more people looking at this in a different light? Let's think for ourselves and interpret the Bible for ourselves.

# OBSERVING HELL

June 25, 2009

THAT WAS THE NIGHT I had a dream about Hell. There was a hole dug in the wall with layers that were red. I knew it was an opening to evil. It was frightening like I wanted so badly for it to be sealed. I went through the hole with someone. A guide that was to my left or maybe behind me. Tall and quiet. A presence. It was like an aerial view of a cliff you'd see somewhere in Europe or Ireland or something. Very very tall and jutted out with super huge waves violently crashing against the rocks at the bottom. It was cloudy. At the top where there should have been grass there were demon things with whips in their claws to keep what seemed, order? . . . There was smoldering. I don't remember seeing actual fire though. No flames but smoldering like lava had passed over it. Along the whole side of this cliff were cages piled one on top of the other. Old dark iron looking cages with 3 bars for openings. Souls, not human formed bodies but deformed things were in each of them. What seemed like knotted deformed fingers were grabbing the bars. I saw no faces of the souls. Male and female seemed not to exist to the souls in the cages. The feeling was hopelessness. Repetitive. But not knowing, no, NOT REALIZING they were in Hell. Over and over and over and over-like that. Constant repetitiveness. They didn't even seem to be present. Trapped in their minds of no escape would be a good way to describe it. Whatever had made their soul go to this level is what they kept thinking about. Like it consumed them. It was very dreary and creepy. I was looking at all of this like flying from right to left then standing on a tall hill overlooking it all with this guide. And I remember pointing to it and said, "If that's Hell, I do NOT want to go there!!!" with my arm pointing to it and facing the guide. Then I was hugged. My cheek on white linen. An angel I can only assume. But that hug told me everything was ok. And then I was "brought back".

# PURGATORY

I HONESTLY DIDN'T BELIEVE IN it. My friend and my grandmother unfortunately killed themselves. I have gotten signs from them so I know that they are ok and not sitting somewhere in limbo. So I never believed there was a purgatory. But there is. Shortly after I was brought to Hell to observe I had a dream about Purgatory. But here is WHY one would go to Purgatory. To love God. To accept God into your heart. Choosing to follow God. The best way to describe Purgatory is there were cement slabs. 3 levels high. Like underground catacombs. There were souls in there laying next to each other on their stomach—feet in first—heads out. Like you'd cook fish sticks or something. I know, goofy way of putting it. EACH and EVERY one of them had these scary, horrified, bug-eyed, mouth gaping open, expressions. And the ones that were not laying on the slabs were walking around zombified. They were bumping into each other and not even realizing they were and then bouncing off again like one of the first games for a computer or Atari that was tennis. Slow and bouncing off. They had NO clue that anyone else was there with them. I wasn't scared though. I felt compassion for them. So I actually started praying the Hail Mary and the Our Father in my dream. Over and over and over moving my arms and hands for one of them to see me and hear me and repeat after me the prayers. A couple of them did. I'm pretty sure that was what it took for them to be saved. And I woke up.

# HOW DO YOU TELL YOUR PRIEST THAT YOUR KID ISN'T SUPPOSED TO GO TO CATHOLIC SCHOOL??

YOU DON'T. WHEN WE MOVED here to Minnesota I told my husband that I would be open to the kids going to the Catholic school he went to as a child. So I made an appointment to get a tour and check it out. All that went well but the tuition thing bothered me. It cost a lot of money. And the lady said they would work with what we could afford but I would still feel bad not paying all of it and other people paying the full amount. It didn't seem fair. And the fund raising you had to make up the set amount difference out of your own pocket if you couldn't get enough from donations. Lexie didn't like that she would have to wear a uniform because the lady showed us what they looked like. So Kevin and I talked about it that night. We decided not to but when I went to bed I asked God to please let me have a dream to let me know that we were doing the right thing. What did HE want us to do? So that night I had a dream about white. Lots and lots of white. Everything was white and I thought we were talking about white sheets. I didn't see the other person but I heard him say, "why pay for something when it comes for free?" It was spoken very clearly. I woke up and thought to myself, "was that God?" but went back to sleep still needing more direction. Before I awoke I remember seeing Jesus. Yes, Jesus. Holding up a fabric strip with cheetah spots on it. When I woke up I thought that had to have been the craziest thing to dream about!! And then it made sense. He was showing me Lexie's what she calls her, "cheetah girl tights". She couldn't wear those if she went to the Catholic school cause of the uniforms!! So we put her in public school. With no regrets or worries.

# WISE WORDS

You know, Flea from the band The Red Hot Chili Peppers??! THAT Flea. My husband came home to tell me that his brother had told him that Flea had been in town that weekend at a local music store to endorse his new guitar or something. He didn't see the notice in the paper till a day too late. Kevin told me he had something to tell me that he knew would, "make me cry". He was right. He left to go to a friends house after he told me and I started to cry. If only to meet Flea, to sit and listen to him play. It would have been so awesome. This coming from the girl that when she went to her first concert of theirs I started crying when they were putting up Chad Smith's drum set. Their music has made a sad girl happy many times. Thank God for them. Anyways. I started to think, what would I even say to Flea IF I had met him?? Then I knew. "Flea, I am not bitter anymore." When my ex and I divorced I found a quote from Flea that I wrote down that would remind me of HOW I wanted to be someday. It read, "when I am old and a grandpa I hope to . . . . have lots of love in my heart and not be bitter just be forgiving and full of joy and love". I have kept it for 5 years now. And I stopped crying and feeling sorry for myself for not meeting him and thought that maybe someday I'd get a different chance. Then I opened up the Bible to read in a random spot like I did every night and it was Ephesians 4:31 that read, "All BITTERNESS, fury, anger, shouting, and reviling must be removed from you, along with all malice. And be kind to one another, compassionate, FORGIVING one another as God has forgiven you in Christ."

Right ON!!!!

# A GRASSHOPPER RELAYS
# A MESSAGE

SEPT. '09 I NEEDED TO get out of the house and find something to do with my time so when Father told us they needed volunteers for teaching religion class I called up the woman in charge to do just that. There were 4 spots open. I was super excited! She asked me which grade of those I would prefer to teach. I wasn't particular. Any. I told her my daughter would need to be in the 1st Communion class also. She asked me about her and if she was baptized because she needed to be before April when 1st Communion was. I told her that neither of my kids were yet. She told me she would stop by and drop off the itinerary I would need for my class in my mailbox because she was sick with the flu. But nothing came. Two weeks went by and I hadn't heard from her. Then I saw her at church on Sunday. Religion classes were set to start that week. She was ignoring me. So I approached her after church. I said, "well, I guess you have all the teachers you need cause you haven't called me at all or brought out the stuff you said you'd drop off". She said she would like me to be a helper for the 2nd grade class. Ok . . . . then she questioned me about my kids baptism plans. I told her I was waiting for my friend that lived in Green Bay to be able to come as she would be my sons god mother. Then this woman tried to force me into getting them baptized THAT day. Right that very minute. Have someone from the church stand in for all the god parents. I could feel my face getting red. I told her no, that I would wait but I heard, "today—it's SO important!" as she followed me out into the lobby. Making me feel like a terrible mother for waiting 7 yrs and 4 yrs. Even Kevin was surprised at how pushy she was. I went outside where everyone was having donuts and orange juice and took Father aside and told him what had just happened. He was surprised. His eyebrows shot up when I told him she wanted to do it right now. He said no, that it was fine when we were ready to to just let him know. He was all cool with it. So I went home and opened up the newsletter. STILL in need of volunteers . . . . search your heart to share . . . . blah, blah, blah . . . . Apparently I wasn't GOOD ENOUGH to teach, according to her standards. I sat on my steps with my bible in my arms and started to cry. I couldn't believe what had happened. She totally judged me. I took my bible and a blanket and went up into the pasture to read. I would feel better sitting in the grass with the clouds above my head. The birds in the huge Cottonwood tree we have were Really loud. There were flocks of red-winged blackbirds. The verse I opened to-random of course—was how God takes care of the birds-so imagine me! Then the kids came and sat down on the blanket with me. A little green grasshopper hopped over. I was able to pick him up-hold him-pass him to Adam-Adam pass him to Lexie-and back to me again. Funny how he just sat and kissed/nibbled our hands! Friendly little guy! So I told the kids how God sent the locusts. I looked it up and read the story in Joel to them. It even says to tell your children that story. :) They then got up to play. I kept reading to Chapter 3. Prophesy, dreams and visions. It made me feel better. I've been aware of my special gifts since my senior year of high school. I should believe in myself-the path God is giving me. So again, randomly, I chose another reading. Acts 2:11 The Mission in Jerusalem. Peter gave his speech quoting Joel. What I had JUST read! I shouldn't let what others say/do against me bother me. God believes in me. It doesn't matter what anyone else thinks.

# THE WOODEN ALTER REVEALED

October 22, 2009

CLASSES HAD STARTED FOR RELIGION with them still needing volunteer teachers and I was supposed to be the helper in my daughter's 1st Communion class. That lasted 2 times and then another mother, which I think was the plan from the beginning, took over to the handing out of things and listening to the kids say their prayers for their prayer board. I was just a mom coming in to sit next to my daughter. I felt pretty stupid. I had been ousted even from helping. The lady that was in charge of everything had called our house to pester me about the kids baptism plans AGAIN. I could get a proxy, substitute someone from the community to stand in for my friend. Umm . . . no, I already told you I didn't want to do that. I told her I wasn't worried about it which was met by silence. This chic really thought my kids were going straight to Hell if they died that minute without being baptized. Jesus was in his 20's when he finally was! God watches over them. I called Kevin at work and told him and he was sick of her harassing us. So I called and left a message for Father to call me. I would take care of it. Talk to Father and calm down. Two nights later in Lexie's class they talked about, guess . . . . BAPTISM! Yep. And the teacher said that ANYONE can do it as long as it's in the name of Jesus Christ and you don't need holy water. Well, a light exploded in my head. I went straight out to, let's call her Betty, and said, "Mrs. H just told us that anyone can baptize if it's in the name of Jesus. I didn't know that! So I am going to go home and baptize both my kids myself so you won't have to worry about it anymore". She let out a huff and said all flustered, "well, they are going to need certificates if they want to get married in the church someday. It has to be done by Father. I am going to have to call him and tell him this." I said, "Oh, I have already left Father a message to call me. And we will when the time is right. Kevin and I have talked about it and would like you to mind your own business. You have judged me and underestimated the spirituality we have in our house." And she goes, "let's be Christian about this". HA! I replied, "oh, I am choosing my words politely, I could say it a lot different." Pretty much shaking the whole time I was so mad. And even threw in a "thanks" as I turned and walked away. God gave me the correct words to say. I was as polite and professional as was needed. The look on her face of shock was priceless. I don't think anyone has ever stood up to her before. It felt AWESOME! When I got home that night I did a karate chop and kick in the middle of the living room. I relate it to when Uma Thurman took out Darryl Hannah's eye in the movie *Kill Bill*. Swift and accurate. That night I had a dream. The very same night I told Judgmental Betty to mind her own business. In my dream I saw the white cloth pulled from off the alter-revealing the dark stained wood underneath. Not being covered up. To me this means The Truth. What God really intends. Kevin's alarm woke me up. The song playing, *Knockin' on Heaven's Door* by Guns N' Roses. No shit.

# IT'S NEVER TOO LATE FOR ANYONE

JAN 2010 THE KIDS IN Lexie's religion class were learning about confession. It was pretty over the top how it was being pressed on them. It was getting harder and harder to sit with them and not agree with so much. But when we left I would explain to Lexie how I thought things really were that I didn't agree with. Just so she could have another point of view. The last few classes I didn't even go to because it was bothering me too much. They would practice confession and what the priest would say. Mrs. H must have had them repeat, "For he is good and his mercy endures forever" from the blackboard 10 times. I had never heard that before but agreed. That night I read the Bible-opening to a random spot- to the Old Testament-leafing through, chunks at a time-till it "felt right" to stop and read where I ended up. Right in the Bible where it says, "for He is good and his mercy endures forever."

# RECONCILIATION-IT'S ALL ABOUT YOUR HEART

Jan 2010

WE WENT TO GREEN BAY the weekend of Lexie's 1st Reconciliation. She was adamant that she didn't want to do it. I wasn't going to make her but knew in the back of my mind that they had it at 3 at the church my grandma went to if she changed her mind. My mom and I went out for a drink Friday night after we got into town at Brett Favre's Steakhouse. On the way back to her house on the corner by the Packer stadium a man was holding a sign. It read, "Jesus Christ died for your sins . . . something . . . reconciliation". I had never seen anyone like that before. Here, I had really been hoping Lexie wouldn't want to do it. I just thought it was not necessary for a 2nd grader. Me, yes, I have gone to confession a few times and cried afterward. I've done my share of bad things. It feels good to get it off your chest. Kevin thought she should. I was blaming this on his strict Catholic upbringing. That night I had a dream. A young black haired good looking priest was telling Lexie and I about confession in the back of a church I didn't know. Adam was with us but the priest said he was too young. He was very kind. All I remember him saying to us was, "It's all about your heart." I woke up knowing that we needed to go. Kevin had been right. So later that day when we got up to my grandma's up North, Lexie and I went down to the church. It was just us and 2 other people in there. She looked very nervous so I said I would go first to make her feel better and when I came out she could go in if she wanted to. I will tell you what I confessed. I told the priest that it's really hard to be able to visit with my grandma and listen to her stories over and over again and sit in the smokey house that makes me sick and be bored sitting at the table. I knew I shouldn't feel like that. He told me love is the greatest thing on Earth but sometimes it can also be the hardest. I left the confessional and keeled down crying because I felt bad for not being as patient as I could be with my aging grandmother who is an awesome lady. Lexie was milling around quietly and nervously and then went in. It was the most special moment I've ever shared with her and she wasn't even next to me. A very quiet, private, peaceful moment in a beautiful, meaningful church. I had forgotten that I was baptized in that church. My parents and aunts and uncles were all married in that church and my grandma Carlin, who is in Heaven, used to sing in the choir up in the balcony of that church. That night Lexie was up laying in bed when I came to bed and asked, "Mom, can we confess whenever we want to?" "Yes" "Good cause I wanna do it again. This Father didn't tell me to do anything." Meaning her penance. It was so sweet. And you know, I had the very best weekend I have ever had with my grandma that weekend. I was loving and patient and helpful and really lived in the moment with her. I had fun with her. Sunday we went to church together, the kids and I and Granner. Afterward I went around taking pictures of all the beautiful stained glass windows and statues. I really love that church. As I took the picture of the statue that stands above and to the left of the confessional door (who I think is supposed to be St Ann) my camera asked, "did someone blink?" :)

Today is June 13, 2011

After I FINALLY just noticed at church this Sunday a little statue of her, I learned the name of the statue that blinked for the camera. She is Saint Thérèse of Lisieux—The "Little Flower".

# THE LORD FOLLOWS US . . . EVEN ON OUR HONEYMOONS

THE DAY OF THE EARTHQUAKE in Haiti Kevin and I were in Jamaica on our honeymoon. Not surprising it was cloudy and rained all but one day the week we were there. It had rained on our wedding day also. So much that is was called the Million Dollar rain by the farmers because there had been a drought until that day when it POURED out. They say rain on your wedding day is a blessing. Well, God must have really been happy for us that day!!! So Kevin and I went to Jamaica and we had a good time. We didn't let the rain get us down. Kevin says we would have had some bad sunburns anyways if it had been sunny. :) We also made an awesome friend that we keep in touch with that works at the resort we stayed at. So the day of the earthquake we were up in the Blue Mountains on a bike ride. We had a good time and on the way down there was a van in front of our bus that had a bumper sticker that read, "The Lord Shall Provide". I read it out loud and said, "I agree with that." When we got back to our room Kevin had a voice mail on his phone that he had left behind about a job offer and they wanted an interview! He had applied maybe 7 months before and was told not to even bother cause they weren't hiring. But he did anyways. And he got the job once we came home. It wasn't the position he wanted but it's even better. God really picked a good one! The pay is WAY better there and the health insurance rocks and he's a lot closer to home now too. So when he says He will provide He really will, when the time is right. We all just need patience.

# THE SILVER CORD

I DIDN'T KNOW ABOUT THE Silver Cord until reading a Sylvia Browne book and I just saw it mentioned in a James Van Praagh book also. I didn't really believe it myself. One of those things you'll believe it if you see it type of thing. But anything is possible so I keep an open mind. It talks about the silver cord in the Bible. Ecclesiastes 12:6 "Before the silver cord is snapped and the golden bowl is broken." Relating to life and death.

I saw my silver cord on my birthday last year in a dream. It was my present from God. Along with helping a woman IN that dream. I was at a beach house sitting on a porch with light colored wood for the floor and there was lots of white sand when you stepped off the steps. There was a woman to my left and a woman sitting across from me with blond hair. I had seen her walking on the beach crying and now she was sitting in front of me. She was telling me that she, "must have cried for 9 hours the day before so she was walking the beach to think". She told me she was a new mom and couldn't understand why she would be crying so much. I told her that it was perfectly normal. I was a mom of 2 and you have those days but everything will be ok. Then I looked up and saw 2 beautiful rainbows in the sky. I pointed to them and told her that those are a sign from God that everything will be ok. And then I was standing on the edge of the water. Alone. It was pitch black out but the moon was full and shining beautiful on the water. I looked down and saw my silver cord attached to me and was then immediately yanked, pulled up and out over the water. A very graceful flying but fast, very very fast. Being pulled by that cord.

I didn't remember the dream until halfway through the day when I was talking to my husband on the phone. It all started to pour out of me. Helping the unknown woman . . . seeing my silver cord . . . I started to sob at the amount of love and gratefulness I felt. It was really amazing. My feet were even tingling when I was remembering it!! My dream I really feel was real. I know that that woman on the porch of that beach house came away from our meeting with a sense of relief. I really feel that I helped her. I guess seeing my silver cord is proof that it really DID happen.

# SATAN

June 20, 2010

LAST NIGHT I HAD A dream that I was going to be killed by this black haired beast. At first I thought it was some sort of baboon because of the long snout, mouth and teeth. But it wasn't that or a type of monkey at all. The teeth were very sharp and I had grabbed it's upper and lower jaws and was keeping it's mouth open so it couldn't attack me. We were standing out in the middle of nowhere on this very large black rock. Basically having a stand off. And then the next thing I remember is standing next to an elevator. The beast sitting to my right and Satan standing in front of us telling the beast that he was not allowed to hurt me. And he wasn't scary. He looked just like the mummy does in the movie, *The Mummy* with Brendan Frasier. And no, I hadn't been watching that movie before I went to bed. But he wasn't the decomposing scary being. He was what the mummy looked like when he was in complete man form. Egyptian looking with the black eye liner. I didn't feel threatened at all. I told my husband about the dream this morning. He says, "that's f*cked up." He says that maybe Satan has a plan for me. Or else God is watching over me pretty closely because he's having Satan watch over me too. It makes ME think that maybe Satan really isn't bad. Maybe God just put him in charge of the evil doers. After all, he WAS an angel. Maybe he still is . . .

July 2, 2011

I haven't picked up the Bible in a very long time. Today after reading through all these I felt like opening it up. This is what I randomly opened it to. Job 5:23 "You shall be in league with the stones of the field, and the wild beasts shall be at peace with you." Whoa.

# THE SMALL STUFF

ONE OF THE BEST MEMORIES I will have of my dad and I is us looking for neat shaped driftwood last year in Menominee, MI along the shore by the marina. Kevin wished he had a camera because he said we looked like two little kids. My dad always comes up with silly descriptions of what he finds. I found a piece that looked like a tree frog that day so I keep it in my purse as a reminder of the fun we had. When Kevin and I were on our honeymoon in Jamaica I was looking for cool rocks and shells to bring home. Sticking out of the sand I found one that looked like a perfect little foot. With the big toe sticking up, even. Immediately I yelled, "I found one for my dad!" So when I saw him next I gave it to him. To me, it was the most important gift I've ever been able to give him because it was God's way of letting me know that even though my dad and I don't see eye to eye on some things it's the little things that are important. We will still love each other. He was the one that gave me the Footprints poem poster so it was perfect that he should get a footprint rock.

# OUR BUDDY, JESUS

ONE NIGHT LAST NOVEMBER I went to bed earlier than my husband. What he told me the next morning made me laugh. He said that when he came to bed and laid down I came out of my sleep sort of laughing that Jesus was playing with me and he is funny. I remember feeling like a little kid again when he told me about that. Maybe a week after that I had a dream that I was in a bathroom that was all white. I was standing by the sink and mirror and Jesus was sitting by the door on a chair and we were talking-like you would to a girlfriend before you both go out for the night. Maybe Mary was standing to his left . . . I can't remember for sure. But I don't remember what we were talking about. And then a couple of days later I awoke to go to the bathroom repeating, "I get it Jesus, 3, I get it" Then said my prayers that are taped to the mirror. "I am ready." "I am grateful for all that you are and all that you allow me to be." "Please make me an instrument of thy endless abundance". I am still trying to understand what he meant by 3. I must not have really "got" it. Yet.

# A TRUE AWAKENING

June 2010

THIS WINTER AS I DROVE Lexie to her religion class I was crying. She asked me what was wrong. I told her I didn't have any friends. Just God to talk to. I dropped her off and went to the church to sit and be still—looking for comfort. I had never done that before. Fifteen minutes later the choir came in to rehearse so I took off. I drove to the gas station and got a coffee. The dude at the counter was pretty nice. We talked a bit and I drove back to the St. Anne's school to wait outside for Lexie. I tried calling a friend in Green Bay but got her answering machine. So I talked to that. I told her I was lonely and the only real conversation I've had in a while was with the guy at the gas station. I didn't let on I was crying. She didn't call me back. Moving is hard on friendships. Except for having my husband and kids and a Sunday 10 min phone call with my Grandma I was alone for my first 1 1/2 years here. I spent a lot of time crying and missing my friends in Green Bay. A lot of time talking to God. Praying. Reading. But I always told myself there had to be a reason for it—all of the loneliness. I had volunteered to teach religion and they didn't want me. Was ousted from being a "helper" in class. I'm not part of the "grown up in this town" click so when the parents had to meet for my son's kindergarten round up I was the second person seated in the gym. All the tables filled up with everyone sitting near people they know. Mine got filled last. I tried to start a conversation with the two ladies that sat by me that were talking together. I asked if they knew if it was an all day kindergarten because I was new to town. They said yes and continued on with their conversation. It was pretty terrible how I felt. The moms and dads that pick up their kids from Lexie's class all talk out in the hallway. I stand alone. I can say a few words but they seem to not want to bother. Anyways. You get the point. It's hard to be an outsider. So this inner knowing of it all being for a reason got me through. With no lack of tears though. Two days after the kindergarten roundup March 7—I wrote it down—I was upstairs in the afternoon folding clothes in my bedroom. The kids were upstairs in Adam's room down the hall playing. I heard knocking like someone was at one of the doors but I couldn't tell if it was the front or back door. I came downstairs and checked both but no one was there. I asked the kids if they heard it and they said no. So I knew, it was Jesus again. So I said, "Jesus, if that's you, you are welcome to come in anytime you want!" That night I was praying next to my bed and realized that Jesus and God really ARE my best friends. Yes, I think of them as 2 separate people. :) I realized that I needed to rely on them for friendship and love. To open up to them. And I started to sob. It was a true awakening. It was magical and wonderful!! I was so excited!! It WAS all for a reason . . . the very best reason in the whole world! And it was all worth it—so that I could become aware of the relationship that God wanted to have with me. It wasn't mean that I went through that heartache . . . it was a lesson I needed to learn . . . to get me to that next level of spirituality. The next day when I woke up I felt AWESOME!! My heart had been cleansed and I wasn't sad or lonely anymore!!! I didn't feel bad at all! It was truly AMAZING! And that night at one of Lexie's sports things one of the mom's started to talk to me! I can still go a good week without talking to anyone but my husband but it doesn't bother me. I've got God that has filled my heart and I walk around grateful and thankful for everything in my life-even the obstacles. I find even the smallest bug amazing. Everything is so simple.

# THERE ARE NO COINCIDENCES

Everything happens for a reason. The post I wrote about yesterday about God's friendship I had been putting off as my last thing I had to talk about until God gives me something else to write about. Today at the swimming pool I started talking to a mom next to me. Turns out she's new to town also. About the same amount of time I am and she doesn't have anyone that she knows here either for a friend. We blabbed the whole time. It was fun. We have a lot of the same interests. You know when you meet a person and can tell that you get along with them and not in a fake way? That's how it felt. She's cool. So it looks like I might just end up with a real friend here after all. Good timing God. And it's totally supportive of what I wrote yesterday. High Five! Thank you.

# BROKEN

In the picture: Happy with his arm around Bear Bear. A brother's love.

June 30, 2010

TODAY HAS BEEN QUIET POSSIBLY the roughest day in a very long time. This morning one of our kittens (the only gray cat we had-4 others being black and 1 that's white) was run over on accident. It must have been up in the engine and when it jumped out landed under the tire of the truck. It's head was crushed so it was instant. For that I am grateful.

So we buried her. This afternoon I was laying out in the yard and I felt a bite on my arm so I brushed at it and a little tiny grasshopper with a black stripe down it's back was sitting there. I had broken it's leg. Grasshopper always brings me a message from God so I started crying. Silent tears rolling down my face. I told him I was sorry. I told God that I could not kill it. That was his job if it was to die. Not my decision. I picked him up and he sat on my finger than I put him on a blade of grass where he sat there licking his foot and trying to make his leg work. I kept asking him what was the message he was sending me. Then about 20 minutes later I got up to get some water and heard one of the kittens meowing for help. So I followed the meow to under my peonies bush. There sat little black Bear Bear. I laughed at him cause he was behind the little fence I had up and couldn't jump over. So I carried him back up to the porch and set him down. And then I saw that his rear hip and leg were limp and he was pulling himself along. I knelt over him and cried like a little kid. He must have also been run over but is still alive. He is very calm. It must be a spinal injury so he doesn't feel anything. This is why God sent me the grasshopper and I broke his leg. But it still doesn't seem fair. God has his reasons though. I will give him a day to see how he does. Otherwise I know that Kevin will have to kill him. I could not do it myself. And I don't want him to suffer. I pray it doesn't come to that. Little Bear Bear is so sweet. His twin brother Happy is out on the porch laying next to him giving him kisses and meowing at him. I layed my hands on him sending him green healing light. I can only hope for God to fix him. I went and checked on my little grasshopper. He was still sitting on the blade of grass where I left him. I tried to pick him up but he jumped away. Which was a hopeful sign. He can jump. Bear Bear's whole left rear end is limp. I pray for a miracle because the Lord is good to all, compassionate to every creature. Even if it's a little black cat.

# LEAP OF FAITH

WHEN I LIVED IN GREEN Bay I worked at Bank Mutual before going to Associated Bank. They had hired a new boss for our branch and I got bad vibes from him on top of him being rude to each and every one of us girls. He brought out the worst in me. I would get so mad at him I would start to cry and shake like I was freezing to death. It wasn't good. I was planning on just staying there until my house sold so I could move to Minnesota. Just ride it out there. One morning I went out to service the ATM machine and there was a little grasshopper on the door handle. I was careful to open it without disturbing him. Then the NEXT morning he was there again. Odd I thought. Later in the day my friend Steph that worked at Associated told me they were hiring and that I should apply. I didn't really want to start a new job if I was "hopefully" moving soon. I went to lunch and on my way back into the building as I was walking to the front doors a big old grasshopper jumped out of the bushes and landed on my skirt. Ok. He had my attention now. So I went home and read what grasshopper means in my book by Ted Andrews, <u>Animal Speak</u>. Grasshopper means take a chance, take a leap forward. So I filled out an application and turned in a resume at Associated. I got an interview and the job I had applied for had already been filled but I was liked so much that they actually MADE a position and put me in it. It worked out perfect. I was able to leave that negativity at Bank Mutual. Looking back, my old boss was probably put there for a reason so I wouldn't have a problem leaving. A good obstacle to overcome. My new boss was awesome. A really great guy that I really respect a lot. He allowed me to take my lunch and go get my daughter from school and drop her off at her daycare. I was paid a heck of a lot more. Had the weekends OFF to spend with my kids AND I met one of my very best friends, Barbara, working there. I ended up working there for over a year yet until I finally moved to Minnesota. I was even able to get my other friend, Christy, a job there when I was asked to take a promotion by my boss. I told him to please give her an interview because she's super smart and learns fast. She got the job. She's doing great there and has moved up in the company since then. So I was able to help another person which is really cool. Part of God's plan also I'm sure. God made sure to put me somewhere that worked best for me and my little family and my friend—a place where I was HAPPY. Thanks to his little grasshopper.

# ARK—ACTS OF RANDOM KINDNESS

I KNEW I'D GET AN *Evan Almighty* reference in here somewhere!! :)
This weekend I was in a political discussion with my cousin and his
girlfriend. I don't pay much attention to politics really since giving up
my hatred for George Bush years ago. I still cry every time they have
an In Memory of a fallen soldier. I was so mad at George years ago that
I sent nasty, smart ass emails to the White House, put stickers on my
car and hated him 24-7 it seemed. It consumed me. My breaking point
was when I heard the story of the young soldier that gave up his life to
actually SIT on a grenade that had fallen into his Hummer to save his
fellow soldiers. It tore me up. What a brave young man! So I went to
the park and asked God to take away my hate for George. I didn't want
it anymore. Later that day I offered to get the mail down the street for
work. And wouldn't you know, a Hummer drove right past me. And
from that moment on all hatred I had for the war and Mr. Bush was
gone. I decided to do good deeds in name of the fallen soldiers to try
and make up for their lost lives. So, this discussion I was having with
my cousin was about some guy running for office in Wisconsin. Some
self—made millionaire that is supposed to be awesome . . . says my
cousin. What I wanted to know was WHAT does he do with his millions
of dollars that he makes besides fronting his own campaign?? What kind
of a PERSON is he? HOW does spend his millions of dollars because
millions sitting in the bank is useless and you can't take it with you when
you die. How many people is he trying to help with all of his money?
How many lives can he help change? Does he give to organizations?
Does he pay for the other person in lines groceries at the grocery store???
And at this question, my cousin's girlfriend responded . . . "what if that

person is a Dick??!" Perfect!! What if he is? What if you pay for that persons groceries doing something nice for him and it totally changes his outlook on things? What if he goes home to his family and is NICE to them even for a night? How many people can benefit from you doing a nice thing for someone?? Then you've got a lot of people in good moods! And what if he's only being a dick because he is having a hard time making ends meet and you just helped take that burden off his back for even a day, or week, or 2 weeks till his next grocery store trip. Imagine the possibilities of doing acts of random kindness!! I once heard that when you die you review your whole life and how you get to see and feel how you have treated others and the cause and effect of it all. It's a chain reaction and I'd love to see more people excel in the grace of giving. Even if it's holding a door open for someone.

# WOW GOD! THAT WAS FAST!!

August 2010

AN ANSWER TO MY PRAYER for something that happened on Wednesday. I wasn't worried but I have been praying to God for, well, confirmation. Thanks for Father's homily, Lord. We haven't been to church in maybe 2 months but I'd say it's closer to 3. When we were getting out of the truck to go inside Kevin said he felt bad for not coming more but I had a feeling we were right on time. I needed to go there to be close with the Lord, even though I feel like you can be close with him anytime you want . . . it's just different stepping into a church. You see, without going into too much detail about the private thing that had happened this week, having to do with the kids, Kevin had asked me what was wrong this morning. A look of sadness was on my face. Some people are not how you wish they could be. Instead of being honest and loving they say the darnedest things that hurt and point fingers at everyone else. When I told Kevin what was bothering me he made a good point and looked me right in the eye with sincerity. He said, "That's right! We HAVE taught our kids everything they know. We are trying to teach them how to be good people." And then on the way into church Adam, my 5 yr. old, was saying how he was going to share his parade candy with Kevin. He was going on and on about it and was very excited to share because Kevin was going to be at work while we went to the parade today. Father's homily was about teaching our kids to be good. Teaching them to be honest. Teaching them generosity and not greed. We don't need people that are greedy in our lives but to show them love anyways. It was the answer to my prayer. I went up to Father after church and told him exactly that. He said it, "just came to him"—this is what I have been imagining every Sunday—Father praying in the back silently and The Holy Spirit guiding him in what to talk about. Maybe a white light we can't see shining over his head. Or maybe it's more like a pep talk before a big football game. But I don't think Father sings Pants on the Ground like Brett Favre did after mass is over! HAHA! :) Love that!! Maybe others needed to hear that homily also and for me to say it seemed like it was just for my family seems snotty but it was like God was standing there pointing to us. Like he was saying, "there's your answer, Elizabeth." I believe the Holy Spirit DOES tell Father what to say. As with you and me. When we ask, of course. As I write here in my mud room I have some sayings hanging up that say, "My intention is for all of my activities to be directed by Spirit." "My intention is to love and radiate my love to my writing and anyone who might read these words." and "My intention is to trust in what comes through me and to be a vehicle of Spirit, judging none of it." Words from Dr. Wayne Dyer. Part of our nightly prayers with the kids is saying, "Please God, help us Say and Do the right things." All you have to do is ask and you shall receive. I picked a random spot in the bible Friday night. I said, "what would Jesus say?" and I opened it to Mark 9:23 Jesus said, "Everything is possible to one who has faith."

# TAKE THE TIME . . . .

August 18, 2010

I TOLD MY HUSBAND I was going to write today. He asked if something happened. I said, "no". But it shouldn't take Jesus actually knocking on your door to make you realize that God is with us at all times. I looked out my car window at the sky while my 2 kids were in the backseat fighting with each other making me want to pull over and spank them on a 5 1/2 hour ride back home to MN from Green Bay. I was amazed at the beauty of it all. I got the kids attention for them to take a look at it also. All was made calm in the car. When was the last time you took a look at the sky?? How many people are too busy in their daily routine that they forget to look up? The kids and I just got back from a bike ride. I listened to the crickets, watched the pretty little yellow butterflies, paid attention to the sunflowers just growing randomly out in the field, looked at the different shades of purple that the flowers along the road were and looked at my children's faces as they said, "whoosh" as they went past me. I took a mental picture of that. God doesn't have to reach out and physically touch us on the shoulder. He gives us so much beauty in nature and our family members, our pets and friends and even strangers. We just have to take the time to acknowledge that and **ENJOY** it.

# REINCARNATION

I WILL NEVER FORGET 4 years ago when I found in the Bible where it says that Elijah came back as John the Baptist. I called Kevin, who didn't believe me until I read it to him. And then he got his Bible and read it for himself. Last weekend I had a dream that this couple had 7 babies at once. They handed me a little girl and she started talking to me. A baby. But I can't remember if her lips were moving or if it was telepathically. She was telling me all the things she was going to go through in this life. She had learned some lessons in her last life and so this life that she was starting she wouldn't have to go through them again so it was going to be a much easier life. She was excited and happy. It was all planned out. Where she would live at points in her life, who she would meet and love. It was all a big plan. Even the babies that were her siblings she knew already. Like they had planned to all come down from heaven together. Can you look at your own life and the things that have happened to you and the people you have met and see where this could be true?? That things are not just a coincidence. That everything happens for a reason. I have read that deja vu is really your soul's recognition that you are right where you are supposed to be. That you are right on schedule with the plan you have laid out for yourself. I told that to my brother the other day, and for someone who thinks I'm crazy, he actually thought about that. :)

# RAINBOWS

ALL SUMMER LONG I WAITED to see a rainbow. I ran out to the edge of the fields on all sides of our house for each storm in hopes to see one. This is the only one I saw. An extra special double one. What makes it special is that I was sharing it with my friends in Crivitz, WI. We were up there for a "girls weekend" for my friend, Patti's birthday. We had a really good time. And what makes this rainbow so special is that earlier in the day I had run into one of my "favorite people" at the campgrounds bar. Dale Steffenhaggen. I hadn't seen him in almost 10 years. What makes Dale one of my favorite people is that he has a laugh that is 1 in a million. It will amaze you. I have even taught my kids his laugh. It is that special. It goes on and on and on. It's the best. When the rainbow appeared he was at our campsite talking to us. I was able to tell him that he really IS one of my favorite people. I don't think he believed me but it's true. He is a genuinely good guy. And it was important for me to tell him I thought so. It's important to tell the people you know how special they are. No matter how silly it may sound. So whenever I look at this picture I will remember standing there with Dale telling him how funny he is and how God puts rainbows there for us to know that everything will be ok. Did any of you watch The Bachelor this season with Ali? The day that she told Chris that she was choosing Roberto a rainbow was in the sky out of nowhere. It was a sign from his mom in Heaven that he was going to be ok. It literally took my breath away and I started to cry when they showed that. It was special. Not only for him and his mom to have a special moment but for everyone watching that needs "signs" from Heaven.

And to believe in them.

Side note: My friend Patti just told me that there were actually 3 rainbows together that day! I didn't see the other because I hadn't walked over to the clearing with them. I have never even HEARD of 3 rainbows together before!! Awesome!

# MANNERS

LAST WEEK I WAS SICK with a cold and had about lost my voice. Kevin decided that to make an attempt to make me feel better he would take me to Emma Krumbees for lunch. While we waited in line to have the hostess take our name (behind 3 other couples) the man standing BEHIND us in line with his wife went straight up to the hostess stand, literally stuck his face next to the book and got her attention so rudely after he interrupted her with the ladies in front of us, to have her put down his name next. Then walked back to where he stood behind us. I, in my hoarse voice, turned and said, "I CAN'T BELIEVE HE JUST DID THAT!!" It was completely and purposely rude. It made me hot with anger that anyone, especially at his age (maybe 55) would think that they had the right to act like that. I can't remember the last time I bit my tongue that hard. I was fuming. So we gave our names next and backed off to look at the different kinds of breads they had. To my joyous surprise, a GENTLEMAN standing with his wife, turned to me and politely asked if we were in line. And folks, I tell ya, it was like a ray from Heaven was coming down on this guys white hair. It was fantastic! In about 1 minute's time the Lord had shown me that there IS GOOD on the opposite side of bad.

# GOD, OUR COMFORTER

Photo: Bear Bear. The last time I saw him. Sitting in stillness. Letting the sunshine shine on him.

BEAR BEAR, THE BLACK KITTEN, lived for 2 weeks. This is hard for me to write about because I feel such a connection to him. I put so much hope and prayer into him surviving but in the last week knew that he wasn't going to make it. I have an outlook that is different than thinking that my faith didn't work. Cause it's not like that. I constantly prayed for him. I layed my hands on him and tried giving him my strength and energy. I prayed that Angels would ease his pain and hold him in their arms. Everyday all day long I was out there kneeling on the ground next to him. Caring for him. Loving him. Saying kind words to him. Making sure he was getting something to eat and drink. Everything you would do for someone you love. The evening I saw him last he looked so tired. I was outside walking around taking pictures of flowers after I had put the kids to bed and took one of him. It was quiet. I knelt down next to him and gave his shoulders a massage and told him that it was ok for him to go now if he must. He had given such a good fight and was so strong and brave but I wanted him to know that I understood and he was tired. It was time. Sweet little guy. The next morning I couldn't find him. I told the kids he must have went off to die because that's what animals do and that he was ok and in Heaven now. Two days went by. I sat on the cement of the front porch steps and smelled death. He was under the porch. I had Kevin take apart the lattice siding of it to get him out to give him a proper burial. He was far back-just under the door. The kids were up playing in the treehouse. I didn't tell them what we were doing. Best to have them remember Bear Bear how he was before. As Kevin was digging the hole I went to get some flowers. My Lilies were in bloom. I wanted to choose the one that was the nicest. As I went to cut it from the stem I noticed a little grasshopper with a black stripe on it's back sitting on it. The same from the day Bear Bear was hurt. Only a little bigger. I was not surprised to find that. It made me feel good. Peaceful. The grasshopper jumped off and I layed the lily on Bear Bear and we buried him. I went and collected more flowers for the top and Kevin just stood on the porch staring at me. He said he couldn't understand how I could care so much about a little cat. What was the reason for Bear Bear in my life?? In my opinion? Honestly? I kinda feel like I walked in God's shoes. I think a lot of what I went through with caring for Bear Bear was a lot of how God feels about us when we are sick or hurt and are not going to make it. It must break his heart like it did mine. He is with us. By our side. Loving us. Holding our hand so that Time/Fate/Destiny can run it's course and when it does—all of our pain and suffering will be gone and we will be at peace.

# JESUS LOVES CHILDREN

October 2010

TUESDAY NIGHT ADAM WOKE UP just after midnight coughing like he had The Croup. It sounds like a seal barking. He had it when he was 2. He will be 6 next month (I didn't know that children outgrow The Croup)So I started the hot water running in the shower and had him sit in the bathroom to help because that is what I did when he was little-I thought the steam would help. Twenty minutes went by and I had calmed him down from crying but he was still gasping for air saying he couldn't breathe. I turned off the water. I was going to take him outside to see if the cold would help, another Croup remedy, but thought maybe we should really go to the hospital instead. I was nervous. And then, as I stood next to Adam, who was sitting on the floor, a LOUD and I mean LOUD knock came on the door. It startled me. I knew it was Jesus but I still said, "what was that!?" and Adam said, "what?" so I opened the door and went out to the living room and since Lexie had gotten up with him to begin with I thought that maybe she had knocked or thrown something at the door but she was curled up on the couch in a blanket half asleep and when I asked her what that noise was she didn't know what I was talking about. It seriously sounded like someone had thrown a rock at the wooden bathroom door. It was that loud. Jesus wanted me to take him to the hospital. Now. Adam fell asleep on the way into town. I had to grab him by the jacket and give him a good shake because he was unresponsive. It scared the shit out of me. Going to the ER was the right thing because they had to treat him with steroids and antibiotics and kept him overnight for observation. It was a type of

Bronchitis. Adam was such a good boy for the doctor and nurses. He was happy to get help. Not so much when they had to put the IV in though. Understandable because I about fainted myself. Jesus not only made sure that Adam was kept safe and was well taken care of but taught me a lesson as well. Trust your instincts. Especially when it comes to your children. If you think that you should go to the hospital, then GO!

# A LITTLE CRYING NEVER HURTS

I WAS PRETTY SAD A couple days ago. Probably the normal for most people . . . could use some extra money for paying bills . . . cause that is stressful . . . but the other that was getting me down was the fact that I can't lose the 10lbs. I gained 3 years ago from that birth control pill YAZ. I switched from Yasmin to that because the Yasmin was making me very emotional and crazy. I went off them completely 6 months later but I cannot lose the 10lbs. to save my life. The sadness had ruled my world for a good week. And I spent almost the whole day on the couch for a few of those days and it left me very tired and lazy. I usually do a 45 min workout video each day and sometimes will run at least a mile and a half when I feel like it but with not losing even a pound or two I gave up last week in exercising. Two summers ago all I did was run 3 miles a day to get ready for the 5K in town but I still didn't lose anything. Oh, yeah, I even did 2 of Jillian Michaels' videos for a month each with no weight loss and one of them was called *30 Day Shred*! So I have kept active and I basically eat healthy(yes, I DO indulge in sweets, but not too often . . . I can make a bag of Butterfingers from Halloween last for months up in my cupboard :) So when I exercise my body gets all toned and tight and I look great but it's that scale that bothers me. So I was sitting at the lunch table telling Kevin that, "I am sick of exercising and not losing the weight!!" He was telling me how good I look when I do it and how it makes me in a good mood. Which is true. But I was frustrated and since I had given up exercising last week I was kinda on a self destructive-pity path. As I sat at the table a Cardinal was sitting on the branch outside the window. It's not uncommon to see Cardinals and many other wild birds at my house. But this time it was different.

He was staring at me. And when I waved to him he opened his mouth in acknowledgment. I looked up what Cardinal means in my <u>Animal Speak</u> book. It can teach Renewed Vitality through Recognizing Self-Importance. WOW. Cause I felt like shit. I needed to hear that. So I walked over to see what the other birds were doing by the feeder in the living room and there was a dead grackle laying there. Hmmm... I don't get those at my feeders... Grackle's Keynote is Overcoming Excess and Emotional Life Congestion. "It is a noisy, chattering bird and may be a reminder to quit talking and DO something." Wow. These signs from birds had me pegged. God's little Messengers :) So after Kevin went to work I wandered back and forth in my living room and finally ended up kneeling at the couch crying to God how sorry I was to be wanting to lose those 10lbs and I should be happy with my results as they are and I also apologized for asking for money to help pay the bills. I shouldn't worry and things will work out. I was sobbing because I felt like those were silly things for me to pray about when we are very blessed in many ways and I just shouldn't worry. After I got all that out I felt a lot better. I stood up and put in my video and exercised and felt awesome afterward!!! So now I'll keep at it. I guess sometimes we just have to let it all out and give God our worries and troubles and He makes everything better :)

# LIFE SUPPORT

TODAY IS GOING TO BE something that happened this October while I was reading the new John Edward book, <u>Infinite Quest</u> (I really like it!!). Many things happened to me while reading this that were just not coincidences. But the one I want to talk about today is because maybe someone out there reading this is going thru this. Meaning, making the decision to take someone off of life support. Once again this story involves a grasshopper. God's little messenger. I had just started reading this book up in the pasture, in my hammock with my pillow, when I had to come back down to the house for something. As I came back out I saw that Happy, the cat, was batting around a very big grasshopper on the cement patio. A closer look showed that he had not only pulled 1 of it's legs and a wing off but had put a hole in it's stomach. My belief is to never kill anything because it is not MY decision. But looking at this big guy I couldn't let him be in agony like what I'm sure he was. So I stepped on him. What a dreaded feeling. I knew it was the right thing to do but it still made me sad and not happy to have had to do it. I slowly walked back up to my hammock, feeling guilty. But wouldn't you know that the very next page I read is John Edward talking about taking people off life support because we love them and we are just helping them move on and that we should not feel guilty about it. I did NOT expect him to touch on this subject at all. I did the right thing and let my heart guide me. I can only hope that if you or someone that you know is put in this situation that you can look at it from a standpoint of love. Not guilt.

# BLOODY MARY

I'M SURE WE ALL DID this in grade school. It was rumored that if you said her name 3 times in the mirror that she would appear. Well, I was always too much of a chicken to do it and stayed the hell away from those dark bathrooms at school! Now Lexie, my daughter, has learned it at school too. In some ways it's like a 3rd grade right of passage. She isn't as scared of stuff as me. In fact, I heard her repeating this in the shower one night and I snuck into the bathroom and stood listening. About the time she got to the 10th time the whole plumbing system went crazy and started shaking and making noises. She shut up. So when she got out I told her not to say it again. You never know. And I don't want some unwanted ghost in my house! Well, one night I was watching PBS and they were doing a story on The Battle over the Bible or something and they said that Queen Mary I of England was nicknamed Bloody Mary burning some 300 Protestants at the stake because she believed that being Catholic was the only way. I had meant to tell Lexie this story but forgot until Christmas Eve dinner at my husband's mom's house. So here at the kitchen table it pops back into my head when I look over at Lexie making scary faces at the other girls and I tell her to remind me to tell her about the Real Bloody Mary later. Now Kevin's sister says she is going to call me at 3am when her kids can't sleep. Geez. Yeah, I admit it probably wasn't the best time to bring it up but sometimes, try as I might, I don't have a filter. :) SO. We go home and I open up the family tree booklet that lets others in the family know what they've been up to for the last 4 years. All of Kevin's siblings, individual cousins and aunts and uncles and families took the time out to write a summary of their lives. I turned to our page. His mom totally went through what Kevin had written for it and edited out a bunch of stuff. Even my blog address that Kevin wanted in there because he is proud of me. Once again, his mother is a strict Catholic. I didn't expect her to be like this tho. To not even give anyone else the chance to read it and make their own decisions??!! I had happily helped make Christmas dinner with her and had a few nice talks about God and reasons for things and now I read that she took out the blog address . . . among other things . . . important things to Kevin! Kevin's other cousins' website address for the liquor store he runs was kept in!! Does THAT make sense?? And all I can think about is Bloody Mary. How if someone else didn't agree with her views she had them killed. I'm in NO WAY saying his mom would ever do this but can you see the similarity? Not letting others make up their own minds? It's either this way or it's not right?? How can people still have that same mind set????

Here's a footnote: The very next day, Christmas Day, the B Mary reference was brought up AGAIN in Oconto, 350 miles away, when I asked my brother about his friend's crazy ex-girlfriend. I said her name and then Granner, did too and Bob, my brother, goes, "SSHHHHH!! Don't say her name! If you say it 3 times she might appear!" Too funny!!!

# FAITH AND CONFIDENCE

January 12, 2011

TO HAVE FAITH IN GOD also gives you Faith in yourself. Faith and Confidence have gone hand in hand with me these last few days. If you can truly give your problems, worries, anger, whatever it is that is bothering you to God to handle He will. Over the last few days I have been shown that this is true. With amazingly fast results. We are talking the very next day. It's amazing and it sounds unbelievable but it is true. The Lord wants us to come to him when we need him and are sad and confused or when we are thankful and happy. Anytime! So talk to Him. Anger and hurt can be turned into Love. Trust Him. Yesterday as I drove into town to meet Lexie at the school for her field trip I put aside things that were bothering me and gave them to God to deal with. Just told him to take them. I wanted she and I to have a wonderful time and I didn't want my troubles weighing me down. This is something I have always wanted to be, THAT mom that goes on the field trips. My mom always was there with us for ours and I was always so happy and proud to have her with me. Lexie was the same way yesterday. It was great. We had a wonderful time! Even on the bus home there was only 1 seat open towards the back and wouldn't you know, it was the one with the heater so Lexie and I-we love heaters!—snuggled our legs up to it. :) That morning I had repeated to my husband what my dream from the night before was about. Wouldn't you know that 3 things from that dream, I actually SAW on display at the museum we went to?! That gives me confidence in my abilities and myself. It cleared up other things that had been just what I had prayed for. Prayers and love for the others involved in my situation will continue, but as for me, lesson learned to check off my life list—you can only control yourself. Not what others might say or think about you. (I'm sure there will be many times I will have to remind myself of this) But YOU know the Truth and so does GOD and really, that is all that matters.

# MOVING ON—WEIGHTLESS

This photo is from my garden. What is cool is that I have a statue of Jesus behind it that the previous owners left for us. It's so overgrown that you can't see Him but you know He is there . . . I smile at the similarity of it.

"CHOOSE TO ALIGN YOURSELF WITH people who are like-minded in their search for simplified inspiration. Give those who find fault or who are confrontational a silent blessing and remove yourself from their energy as quickly as possible. Your life is simplified enormously when you don't have to defend yourself to anyone, and when you receive support rather than criticism."—Dr. Wayne Dyer

I believe that Spirit will let us know when we are on the right path. And when we pray and ask for guidance if we are unsure of things we will get our answer. My answer came to me two days in a row. For a few months now I have been cutting ties with certain people in my family. All that has come from interaction with them has been heartache and I didn't know if avoiding them would be the right answer. I love them. And because I love them I allow them to repeatedly hurt me. Intentional or not. I just wanted a stop to all the drama and negativity that surrounds me like a dark shadow after they spew their garbage on me. I wanted to take the higher road and if that meant sending them love from afar while avoiding the negativity than that sounded like a good idea. So I have been pretty distant with some people that I used to be close to. It is a conscious decision I made and was wondering if it was the right thing to do. I had some Reiki done for the first time last week. I told her about the negativity that is coming from my loved ones. While she was performing the Reiki on me I had my eyes closed and saw what looked like bubbles coming up from the ocean floor to the surface. I went home and had a very vivid dream that involved my grandmother-that has passed away-giving me a sign of love and support. I cannot express how special this was. That whole next day I was amazed by the meaning of my dream. But for the following 3 days after that I interacted with my husband and my kids like I wasn't me. It was like I was engulfed in a force field of negativity. I was knit picky to all of them and had a totally crappy outlook on life. I didn't understand what was happening to me. The night of the 3rd day I prayed and spoke to my soul in 3rd person. Telling myself that I need to forgive myself for anything I may have done in the past. That I was only doing the best that I could at the time. (I made a lot of very bad and dumb mistakes when I was in my late teens to 20's that I have been reviewing with a friend). I prayed and asked for God to help me be Beth again. Fun, loving, happy Beth. And asked what I should do next. On the 4th day I woke up feeling great. Not grumpy to the 10th degree like the previous 3 days. I got the kids off to school and turned on *The Today Show*. Mackenzie Phillips was just starting to be interviewed. And what she said at the end of her interview was poignant to me. She said that she prays for God to help her speak about her family members with love. That even though her family doesn't support her and believe her she still sends them love and hopes someday they will come back but her 24 yr old son said to her-something like, "But Mom, don't you see how happy we are without them in our lives? Without their drama? We're having fun!" And it was like, DING! She's right. He's right. That's ME! I HAVE been a lot happier since not talking to some of my family members! It's ok and I don't have to feel bad for it! My husband, Kevin, and I went to lunch at Perkin's that day. I laughed so hard my sides hurt TWICE! I haven't laughed that hard and at silly things like that in a long time. And the very next day was the post I have on the top from Dr. Wayne Dyer on Facebook. Sending my family love from afar is ok and I don't have to feel bad about this decision. I can live a simple and happy life. And those 3 days that I walked around grumpy, I think, were the bubbles coming up and surfacing from the Reiki. I got rid of all the crap I have been carrying around for so long—my negativity and the negativity that belongs to others that was placed on me. It won't be bogging me down anymore! Pretty cool, heh?

# ALWAYS TELL THE TRUTH

I'M LAUGHING BECAUSE I SAW Kato Kaelin last week at LAX when we had a stop there on our family vacation to Puerto Vallarta. I thought I would see someone really cool, like one of the Red Hot Chili Peppers and here it was KATO. For anyone that doesn't know who Kato Kaelin is Google him. He was a witness in the OJ Simpson murder trial. Once again, the subject of the Truth has been acknowledged.

# WHAT HAPPENS WHEN YOU FOLLOW SPIRIT'S GUIDANCE???

March 2011

WONDERFUL SURPRISES AND IN THIS case a Dream Family Vacation. I started out the new year wanting to go on a family vacation (because life is short and tomorrow isn't a guarantee) but after checking out Disney World and Atlantis I found that vacations cost a lot of money for a family of four. So I just let the idea go and figured we could try again next year. But last month I had an unknown number on my cell phone that I didn't answer but called it back to see who it was maybe an hour later. Turned out to be a Timeshare pitch for Villa Del Palmar in Puerto Vallarta. I have absolutely NO CLUE how they got my number. I don't give that info out. And don't buy stuff on-line. And I certainly have NEVER gotten a telemarketer call in the 5 yrs I've had this number. I took the info down and then asked the girl what her name was. She said, "Elizabeth". Same as me! This is why I decided to go. And to Puerto Vallarta and THAT resort. Because we had the same name. Sounds crazy but it just seemed "right". So I called up the travel agent and had her book the flight and room, not going through Elizabeth because I wasn't sure if it was a scam or not. I still wanted to be careful. But still got one heck of a deal! My friend, James, had just posted pics of HIS trip to Puerto Vallarta so again the name came up. I asked the travel agent if the whales would be there still so we could see them. She said yes. And the very next day after the trip was booked and we told the kids where we were going and how we were going to whale watch they actually saw a group of kids on PBS tv on a whale watching adventure. It was a sign that we were on the right track. My ex-husband was nice enough to send back permission for the kids' passports quickly because we only had like a month window to work with before we left. Not worrying about them making it on time because I knew it was what we were meant to be doing was so less stressful. To have faith calms nerves. The night before we left I looked in the journal that I keep. It is hopes and dreams. Things that I had written down that, "I am grateful for and blessed because . . . ." (as if they have already happened) and I found that I had actually written that, "I got to go whale watching" and had a Dream Family Vacation with Kevin with us (because he works a lot and I go home to Green Bay, WI a lot on my own with the kids because of this.) I had written, "I would love to go on a family vacation *with* Kevin. Not just the kids and I. Somewhere with warm beautiful weather and big, long beautiful sandy beaches with clear clean blue water. A Dream Family Vacation." I was so excited! I had totally forgotten that I had written all that last year!

We got there safe and sound, and met some really nice people there and on the plane :) Hi to Coen and Efrain! Efrain, we didn't do the zip lines because we chose to relax instead. :) When we booked our whale watching adventure they had actually signed us up for scuba diving and a sort of booze cruise where you might see the whales on your way to the destination. Not what we wanted. We just wanted to see whales. :) Luckily when we got on the boat to go over to the other marina and be dropped off for our tour, I chose to sit in the front of the boat and to my surprise no one else that got on before us did! It looked like a jet boat and if it was going to go fast, I wanted to sit in the front!! It reminded me of when my brother takes us for rides in his boat. Love Bob's boat but it's not a way cool jet boat like this one looked like it was. :) On our way over to the other marina some dolphins came along side and were swimming next to it. The guy had Lexie and Adam and I get up from our seats and lean over watching the dolphins swim. It was so cool!! And the only dolphins we saw. Pretty special. I was talking to him about being excited to see whales and when we got to the marina I asked if we could stay on that boat. He had just 4 seats left. Perfect! So he talked to the other guy from our other one and they let us stay. So we spent 4 hours out on the water following the whales. It was the most amazing, spectacular, awesome, phenomenal thing I have ever seen to see those Humpback whales!! The marine biologist on board said that we were very lucky because she hadn't seen a pod in 15 days because they were all leaving. There were 3 males fighting over a female and we even saw them jump!! To see God's creations like that was something I will never forget. I wish I could do that everyday! And to have only 4 spots left for us to be part of it means that THAT is where we were supposed to be.

Our resort, The Villa Del Palmar Flamingos in Nuevo Vallarta was great! Right on the beach and you could walk forever down it! The weather was perfect! Coen gave us a ride into PV and dropped us off at the boardwalk. Amazing. We had a great day sightseeing and we went into Our Lady of Guadalupe Church and prayed. You know, the statue that my camera asked if someone blinked was there. Just in different colors. What a wonderful surprise! When I was like 20 my friend and I, at night in the dark, would go drive out to Guadalupe Chapel in Oconto, WI, that was an outdoor chapel and sit on the alter and drink and pray for God to send us nice guys. We'd even go there in the winter . . . just drive thru the deep snow and hang out there for a bit. Being in that church in PV was reminiscent of that (although I would never disrespect The Lord by sitting on an alter again). To remember the girl I once was and who I am now. To be amazed and grateful for where I'm at in my life now. What a beautiful crown they have on the church in PV. It's really very beautiful. I brought the picture of The Virgin Mary in the candlewax and gave it to the girl outside to give to the priest for everyone to enjoy. You know, some people look at that picture and right away see Mary but others don't. She did. :)

The kids and Kevin boogie boarded for hours of fun and oh, I almost forgot! It wasn't even the resort I thought we were supposed to go to! I thought we would be downtown at the OTHER Villa Del Palmar IN Puerto Vallarta but the travel agent had booked us for this one! Good thing I hadn't looked online at what the place looked like before and gotten myself all excited! I just figured I'd see it when I got there :) All I knew was that it had a kitchen :) It was a surprise to find that out but

I knew it would be ok and it was! The room was WAY nicer than I ever expected! (It was actually 2 rooms and fancy!)I couldn't believe how cheap we got it for! I had been a little disappointed because I thought that being at the downtown one we would be able to watch the fireworks they set off at night but wouldn't you know, while we were having dinner the neighboring hotel set off a bunch of them that we got to enjoy. :) That was the night we walked over to the other neighboring hotel (on the other side)to see what their dinner specials were and we decided to walk back to our own. As I turned from the girl and started to walk away I had Deja Vu. I even did a double take it was so familiar! Yep. Right where we were supposed to be.

And out the window of the airplane home . . . I saw a rainbow over Salt Lake City, UT :)

# BLACKBIRDS

THERE ARE MANY THINGS I love about the Springtime. Besides the flowers coming up (tulips are my favorite) it's the Blackbirds and Red-Winged Blackbirds that signal Spring is here that are the best. Hundreds turn into thousands by the time all these birds get here. You can watch a flock of them flying across the sky and there are so many of them that you can't see where they stop on BOTH ends. As far as you can see they just keep going! I love the song of the Red-Winged Blackbird. It reminds me of when I was little. That and a chickadee's. The birds keep coming in waves and fill the trees and fields. The racket they make is SO loud but when they take off it turns to silence for a split second and then turns to just the sound of many many wings. I love it. They will fly right over your head in a huge black cloud and it's amazing to stand under. The kids and I find this fun-so far none of them have pooped on us. ;) They will stick around for a little bit longer and then fly off to who knows where-it's like when they come here it is their idea of a convention :) and then they will be back to signal the Fall. To watch them soar in their flocks of synchronized flight is amazing. It is like they all have choreographed it. My friend Brandon puts it nicely, "Much like the coordinated flights of the returning flocks, it just reinforces the fact that God made it all, and gave it order, and how connected we are to that order. Brilliant really!" It sure is!!

# PLAN B

April 13, 2011

WE CAME HOME WITH A little souvenir from our family vacation last month. I got pregnant in Mexico :) We have been trying to have a baby for almost a year now. Last week I miscarried the baby. I had never had a miscarriage before. I wanted to be left alone to my thoughts. Kevin made sure that I knew I was loved very much by him. He even got me flowers, donuts and a balloon that read, "Always and Forever". We hadn't told the kids that I was pregnant yet. I had felt like I was Supermom those weeks that I was. We were playing at the park and I was teaching Lexie how to make dinners-really involving her with things that drew us closer together. And Adam loved the attention he got at the park with me alone when Lexie was in her after school program. I was shining. Now I feel like that sparkle is gone. I bawled most of those days last week and then I gave my sadness to God to take from me. I prayed to be allowed to mourn but also to know when it was time to be ok. God has a plan for our family and if that does or doesn't include another baby I accept that. I am doing much much better now. The very next day after I had prayed I went outside to check on my Crocus' that you could barely tell were even coming up the day before but to my surprise about 13 of them were up, making their circle of love and support in the sunshine. I sat there for over an hour thanking God for all life.

Not telling the kids that I had been pregnant and then them not knowing what was going on and why I was so sad had been bothering me. I don't want to keep secrets from them. Kevin was at work and I called to ask him what he thought. He said to tell them if I felt that I should and we both agreed to keep it simple. When I went upstairs to tell the kids, Adam had already fallen asleep. I would tell him the next day. Lexie had a book in her bed laying next to her with the title of, "God Always Has a Plan B". So I opened with that. I asked her if she remembered the week before when she and Adam had so sweetly been sitting on either side of me with their hands on my belly asking when we were going to have a baby. (It was the first time they had ever done that). After I asked her this she looked at me in all seriousness and also relief in her eyes and face and said, "I knew you were. I saw the baby's aura and it was pink and white and I knew it was going to die but I didn't want to say anything. It was really excited to come out but it couldn't see us. It just knew you were it's Mommy." This with her sweet little mouth quivering with tears about to cascade down her cheeks. I asked her when she saw this and she said, "a few days before Adam and I were sitting with you." I told her how hard it had been to not say anything to them then because I was so excited. That had been Friday so she must have seen it around Wednesday-the week before I miscarried. Imagine how she felt and she kept it inside!! Then she told me that my Grandma Helen, that has passed, was sitting behind me and told Lexie to tell me, "Don't be sad." I started to cry. And then Lexie said, "don't cry, you're going to make ME cry." And I asked her if Helen had anything else to say and she looked and said, "She's gone now." Talking to Lexie that night wasn't like talking to a 9 year old. It was like talking to my best friend. She handled it amazingly well and is upbeat that there will be another baby. My daughter is wonderful. Both of my children are.

I wasn't sure if I wanted to write about this. It's too personal. But, today on the radio I heard a discussion about abortions and the question of when does life start was brought up. Does life start at conception? Many questions, many opinions from all of us adults but from a 9 year old little girl, that has been answered. Even in the first few weeks of pregnancy LIFE EXISTS.

# THE VIRGIN MARY ON
# GOOD FRIDAY

Lexie's drawing of Mary

May 1, 2011

On Good Friday I was told about The Shrine of Our Lady of Good Help, located 1 mile East of Champion, Wisconsin by my good friend Laurie during a psychic reading she was giving me. It's not that far out of Green Bay, going towards Sturgeon Bay, so the kids and I went out there. The Vatican has recognized it as a legitimate place where The Virgin Mary has been seen. The kids wanted to stay in the car while I went in so I let them but after I had went down into the crypt and saw and felt how cozy and special it was I went outside to get them. It was cold and rainy outside but inside there were all these purple and white candles burning and it was so quiet and peaceful. While Lexie and I were looking for the spot to put our donation for getting our blessed rosary's I hadn't noticed that Adam had gone to the glass case that held the statue of Mary holding Jesus after the Crucifixion. When I looked over I was shocked to see that Adam was kneeling and in prayer with his hands together in front of his face, eyes closed. Motionless and still. I have never seen him do this. I once saw Lexie do it last Fall after Adam had fallen off a tree and caught his leg in it and was dangling. I thought he had broken it from the way he was hanging there, but luckily he hadn't. I went running to him and when I turned around here she was, kneeling in a pile of leaves just like Adam was now on this bench, both like little angels. No promptings from me, just on their own. I will hold these two memories dear to my heart forever. When I saw Adam, Lexie and I went and knelt next to him. He opened his eyes and looked at me. They were glossy. I thought, "is he going to cry??? Holy cow". Then we all stood up and Lexie asked me if I heard whispering. No, *I* couldn't. We were the only ones down there and there was 1 lady that was upstairs in the church sitting in a pew. Lexie described what the whispering sounded like, using her hands to make actions of voices but couldn't understand what they were saying. I suggested that we all go up to the Mary statue and pray together in front of it. So all three of us knelt together on the padded bench. Then Adam started sobbing. Beautiful tears and sobs of emotion. He looked up at me almost embarrassed and confused and I told him it was ok. That he was feeling Mary's love for him. Pure Love. They talk about people being overcome with emotion at places like this, Lexie and I were witnessing it in Adam. He buried his head in my side and held me tight around my waist. When he stopped crying I pointed out the smell of the Hyacinth flowers at the feet of the angels. It was lovely. Then we all stood up and Lexie pointed to where she had been kneeling. "Look, Mom, it's a M!" I looked down and together we pointed to it and said, "it spells Mary!" A Large M and lower case ary with a very tall and slender cross between the a and the r. Lexie pulled at me and said, "we gotta show somebody!!" But there was no one with us. We were the only ones down there. And somehow I didn't feel the need to. I had left my phone in the car on purpose so I didn't take a picture either. I didn't need to. Then we lit some candles for our loved ones and when we turned to leave Lexie said she saw Mary behind the shrine.

She would like to write it herself. I will let her do the typing now. ok the first thing i saw was mary behind the shrine!It was awsome i couldn't believe what i was seeing.Now i will diskribe her. She was wearing a sute that a nun would where!She had a halo over her head.She had her hands folded.She was praying but . . . i dont know what prayr she was saying.She had blue eyes.Then a coupule of mintus later she left in a cloud of mist.

Minutes to Lexie is really seconds :) She also wants you to know that she had brown hair and a brown rosary around her neck. I have asked her if she is SURE that it was Mary and she is insistent. I have asked her HOW does she know it was her and she just says, she knows. Like it's that simple. She also says that before she left, Mary brushed her hair from her own forehead and itched her brow. Now you can either believe or not believe any of this. It is your choice. I kinda think that the word Mary and the cross were helped made by the young lady I had been talking to earlier when she was leaving and the kids and I were in the entryway. I had given her the picture of Mary in the candles that I had brought with me to Mexico . . . I had 1 copy left from our trip in my purse . . . and she said she had actually been there to Our Lady of Guadalupe. That picture was meant for her that day. She had been kneeling there and praying when I had been in there by myself. I had sat in the pew and thought to myself how sweet she looked in prayer.

I read in the pamphlet that they give out at the church that Mary told Adele, the girl she came to, that she should teach the children to make the sign of the cross. That Sunday my Grandmother and Aunt and I went to church at my Grandfather's Presbyterian church he had been a member of. Not once did the minister make the sign of the cross. Not once. And I didn't see anyone else do it out of the corner of my eye either. This made my heart sad . . . for the children AND the adults. I asked the minister after church why he didn't make the sign of the cross. He looked at me and said, "Huh. You know, I don't KNOW why. You've stumped me." And really, he didn't know. He honestly did NOT KNOW but he took my question seriously. Maybe now they will . . . . I hope so.

# EASTER SUNDAY

As THE KIDS AND I drove home on Easter Sunday back to Minnesota the song, *I Would Die 4 You* by Prince came on. This is my favorite song and favorite part from the movie *Purple Rain*. I was singing along and dancing and we were having a good time when I said, "I wonder if Prince is singing about Jesus?" and then I heard the words, "All I really need is 2 know that U believe." And then I looked up in the sky and straight ahead of me was the sun shining down it's rays of light and two clouds that were equal in length were underneath it but there was a gap between them. If I had drawn lines it would have made a cross. I pointed it out to the kids. "Look guys! One of the clouds is the believers, the other is the non-believers and hopefully SOME DAY they will come together as one." And just then they did just that!

# PERSEVERANCE

(Me on my First Communion, May 5, 1985 with my grandparents and brother. My mom sent me this picture for my 34th birthday last month. Love it!)

A FEW WEEKS AGO I put up the picture of Mary along with this blog address at church on the bulletin board. I was scared up until then what people at church would think of me if they read all this. But when my daughter was being made to cry at school because one of the boys in her class was telling her that she cannot wear the rosary as a necklace because he said it was disrespectful, I decided that now was the time to put up the info for people to read and choose for themselves to believe it or not. I was hoping that this boys parents would see it and check it out for themselves. Since Lexie saw Mary wearing the rosary as a necklace on Good Friday SURELY she wouldn't mind people doing that also.

Today we went to church for the first time since then. And to my partial surprise, someone had taken it down. It was gone. The kids were the first to notice. I had really hoped that I had been wrong when I thought that it wouldn't last long up there. The kids put it up with me. We were all disappointed. I wasn't going to let it distract me from the service. It was Father George's 40th anniversary of becoming a priest. It seems like today I was supposed to be there. The second reading for today, which was supposed to be LAST weeks' reading was EPHESIANS 1:17-23 starts out, "that the God of our Lord Jesus Christ, the Father of glory, may give you a spirit of wisdom and revelation resulting in knowledge of him. May the eyes of (your) hearts be enlightened, that you may know what is the hope that belongs to his call". I held back tears, one slipped quietly down my cheek. I took Lexie's hand in mine and squeezed it. Then Father told the story of when he first started out, how 30 people got up and left the service because he wasn't speaking Latin. He learned that he wouldn't be able to please 1/3 of the people. *I* will only be able to please 1/3 of you that read this. Then they chose to sing *Let It Be,* by the Beatles, per Father's request. The words were printed out for all to sing,

"When I find myself in times of trouble, Mother Mary comes to me
Speaking words of wisdom, let it be.
And in my hour of darkness she is standing right in front of me.
Speaking words of wisdom, let it be.

Let it be, let it be, let it be, let it be.
Whisper words of wisdom, let it be.

And when the brokenhearted people living in the world agree.
There will be an answer, let it be.
For though they may be parted, there is still a chance that they will see
There will be an answer, let it be . . . ."

There are no coincidences. Everything happens for a reason. So I will be making more copies of my pictures of Mary and putting them back up, along with this web address. I will keep doing it as long as it keeps being taken down. I don't make these things up. They are the Truth and people should be able to read it if they want. It isn't up to one person to decide for others whether it is appropriate for them to read or not. God wants me to write, so I do. I don't see why a picture of our Blessed Mother wouldn't be welcome in our church. To me, that doesn't make sense. If the sheet of paper up on the bulletin board that is offering drum lessons can be up there, surely my posting would be welcome also.

After church I asked Father if he had taken it down. He knows about it because I have shown him and told him the story before. He said he did not take it down. So back up it will go. I'm not going to stop.

# SOUL CONNECTIONS

June 9, 2011

THE PICTURE OF MY GRANDPARENTS in the previous post is really special to me. I didn't realize when I put that up that I would actually be talking about my Grandma Carlin now. She is in the light blue colored pants suit. I look at her and I smile instantly. Although she passed away in 1988 when I was 11 years old I am still very close to her. Sunday at church one of the graduation balloons got caught up in the fan WAY above the alter and I'm laughing right now, I seriously thought the church was falling down because Father had the congregation laughing at a story he had told about a man that came to him asking for help because dead people were chasing him at 2am. Kevin and I weren't included in the ones that were laughing. To us, it wasn't funny. He could have been crazy, which isn't something to laugh at, but he also could have really seen ghosts, and to some people that can be very scary! Maybe the way that Father told it gave the impression that it was something to laugh at. I'm sure his initial intent wasn't for people to be laughing at this man. So after we all realized it was a balloon Kevin leaned in to me and said, "it's the dead people." Making their presence known :) And so I leaned over to an acquaintance we happened to be sitting by and told her what Kevin had said. She told me that at her brother's birthday party the day before they had let balloons go and they got stuck up in a tree. I told her that was good luck because that happened when my Grandma Carlin died. We had balloons that we let go and they got caught up in the big willow tree and hung around for a tiny bit than flew away. They were intertwined together to show Grandma and Grandpa's love . . .

that where one goes so will the other . . . and that's how they wish to be remembered. Then I told the woman how when my cousin and I had been talking about the balloons up in the tree many many years later and how the kids had come home with balloons later that same day from visiting their father and when Adam went down the slide the balloon got caught and pulled off his wrist . . . it floated up in my tree above us, hovered for a few minutes and then floated away. What is also neat about that is how letting the kids get balloons was something out of the ordinary for their father. Grandma had somehow had some influence on my ex that day to let them get them. I thought that was really sweet.

Grandma believed in Destiny. To quote my dad in a letter he had written with her before she died that he read aloud to all of us the day of her funeral at the balloon release, that not surprisingly, re-surfaced when my OTHER grandma kept it this long and sent it home with me one weekend from a visit back home. I thought that a copy of it didn't exist and I would never be able to read it. I found it in a pile of notepads she had given the kids. The day the kids and I watched the movie, "UP" together. There are TONS of balloons in this movie. I had to explain to the kids how sometimes we continue to live when our husband or wife passes away before us. I used both my sets of grandparents as an example. That night I found the letter. Ok. Back to what the letter said. "Your mother believed in a destiny. She felt your father was her destiny. You children are offspring of this destiny. This farm and all that it is, is cause of their destiny. All of you children, and your children, exist because of their destiny. Your Mom and Dad/Grandma and Grandpa existed together for 45 years, yet, they felt they had always been together. They believed they will always be together."

I have a window cling that used to be in her kitchen window that says, "You're a very special Mom" on it. I have it on mine. I found it down when Adam was born and we brought him home from the hospital. I had questioned her on how she could have 11 kids! :) It has fallen down when my aunt and uncle and cousins brought the kids sweaters that they had found that she had knitted for all the cousins so they could be handed down. It has fallen down when I had my very first day with the kids on my own when I TRULY FELT like a good mom. And once or twice it has fallen down just to say hi. It is her way of letting me know that she is still around. Monday was my husband, Kevin, and I's 2nd wedding anniversary. I wrote on Flea's (from the Red Hot Chili Peppers) wall on Facebook how the first words I ever said to Kevin I blurted out, "I love the RHCP!" and he said, "me too!" I have no clue why I said that. Then I wrote that it was a match made in heaven. And then wouldn't you know, Grandma knocked the window cling down. At first I thought she was wishing us a Happy Anniversary. Not for a few minutes later did I realize the importance of the timing of it. "A match made in heaven." It REALLY IS! LOL This would be why Kevin and I have always felt a special connection from the first night we met and that we have thought about the possibility of having previous lives together. It's a feeling of belonging and feeling safe with each other that comes naturally.

This must be how she and Grandpa felt for each other also :)

# A BLANKET OF LOVE

I WANT TO TALK ABOUT the power of Jesus' love for us. Two summers ago my new friend told me how she thought her house was haunted. She was finishing up moving into a new house, not because she was scared or anything. She had heard the ghost woman say, "excuse me" to her one night. She felt that this was a "good" ghost. In fact, she believes that this friendly ghost saved her from evil when she was going through a very rough time in her life. She is very grateful to her ghost friend. I said I would come over and see if I felt anything. In the basement I had the feeling of something very hot directly on my head. Like if you were standing under a heat lamp. Then when I went into the living room and the hallway to her bedroom I got goosebumps. None on the back of my neck, because from my previous experience, this means that the spirit is "bad". We left and went to her new home and she had forgotten something at the old haunted one and asked me if I could go back and get it. HA! I knew there would be a reason I'd have to go back on my own :) I was happy to! So when I got in there I started talking to this nice little old lady. I started with saying The Our Father and The Hail Mary. I told her all about how she can come back anytime and visit her home but that Jesus is waiting for her in Heaven and how much he loves her and wants her to be with him. At that moment, it was like a BLANKET OF LOVE was wrapped around me. I could actually FEEL the blanket wrap around my shoulders and it was WARM! It filled me with an incredible sense of PURE LOVE . . . that is the best way to describe it. I had never felt that before. It was amazing!! I wish I could share it with every person. I knew that she had gone and crossed over. I was happy for her :)

# CRYING JESUS

June 12, 2011

THIS MORNING BEFORE I AWOKE I had a dream that I was able to remember and immediately write down. I was in front of a massive church. I was standing with a group of children and their older siblings. I was part of an organization that bought stuffed animals for each of the children (they were from single parent homes). It felt like a Big Brother Big Sister kind of thing. Then we prayed together. To my surprise all of the children knew how to pray. They all got down on their knees and put their hands together. Then everyone left accept my son, Adam and a little black girl. So we walked up the steps to the church. There seemed to be 4 very large bowls that held holy water in them attached to the outside of the building so we put our fingers in the holy water and blessed ourselves before going in. There were rooms that were blocked off with velvet ropes. Like a museum that in each room seemed to be a station of the cross. There were statues in each. When we got to the room with the tomb that held the body of Jesus he came out as a statue carrying the cross on his shoulders and walked past us and 2 tears, REAL tears flew from him and landed on me hitting my leg. It felt like when the priest throws holy water at us at certain times of the year. I was startled and began to cry at the amazement of it. Jesus was leaving. I had the feeling that no one would believe it was him and he was leaving without being seen. But it seemed like he wasn't safe. Like it wasn't safe for him to be in the church. He had to be careful. Then I was pulling into the driveway of a very respected family we have here in town. I went inside and spoke to the Dad and told him about my dream-yes, it was a dream within a dream-all the time I was weeping because Jesus' tears had fallen upon me. It was extremely emotional. He believed what I said and he put his hand on my leg where I said the one tear had fallen. Then I woke up.

# OPPORTUNITIES FOR BLESSINGS

MAY 31, 2011
A page from my Hopes and dreams journal:
I wrote, "I would like to be able to travel at will." For some reason I felt the need to write this down. Then I prayed the rosary and wrote down 3 of the prayer focus' underneath:

Courage
Patience
Perseverance

Three days later I found myself writing down the directions to Hell's Kitchen in Minneapolis to see the band, Adler's Appetite, underneath those words. It was to be my very first trip to the Twin Cities I would make on my own-after living here almost 3 1/2 years and never doing it. God gives us opportunities for what we pray for in unimaginable ways sometimes! :)

That Wednesday Kevin had taken me on a date to Minneapolis for lunch. We hadn't been there for over a year. As we walked out of our favorite Irish Restaurant/Pub to get back to the car and go home, I decided to make a last minute turn to walk towards a shop, the opposite way. To my surprise there was a poster for Adler's Appetite outside a bookstore right in front of us, for Friday (in 2 days!). Kevin and I had seen them back in October and had experienced one of the best rock concerts we have ever been to!! They ROCK!!! If ever anyone has liked Guns N' Roses, you will like these guys! It is formed by Steven Adler, the original drummer for GN'R (who just happened to be my favorite when I had their poster on my bedroom wall in 8th grade)LOL. That night I was so shy when he high fived people afterward that I just stood in awe. Kevin had just finished reading a GN'R book THAT day that I had gotten him from the bookstore. It had been on sale for $5 and I figured he might like it. If he didn't, I would read it just to see how Axl Rose had ruined the band with his ego. We had no clue they were coming to town. This was complete last minute, get a babysitter, we gotta go to this! And this was in a pretty small bar. It was so awesome! I taped some of it on my phone and have been watching it since periodically and smiling and laughing the whole time—we had so much fun!!

So when I saw this poster in Minneapolis I knew I had to have seen it for a reason. I REALLY wanted to go because I knew I would have a good time but Kevin couldn't go because he had to work. I asked people but no one could/wanted go. One of my friends said he could that day, so I was lucky to get a babysitter last minute BUT he found out he had to do something with his family instead. I understood. So since I had the babysitter already I was just going to go to a movie in Mankato-the opposite way from the cities-because I thought I would get lost on my own and it wouldn't be safe downtown since the show got over at around 2am. When I picked up the babysitter I told her parents what I had wanted to do originally and her dad said I should, "think of it as an adventure" and they made it seem like it would be ok to go on my own. The "adventure" idea really clicked in my head. I left the kids and the babysitter at home and started on my way. I didn't want to go to that movie so I took my time driving on the gravel road behind our house, taking the back way and SURPRISE guess what I saw in the field-up close-around 6pm-still lots of light out?? A coyote!!! I had never seen one before, only heard them at night when they yelp when they get something. I stopped the car and we stared at each other. Then he would trot a little farther away and stop and look at me again. He was there for me. There was no doubt in my mind. I was standing outside of my car trying to take his picture and two men drove by me and I heard them questioning what I was taking a picture of . . . I could see him plain as day, maybe they couldn't or weren't supposed to!

From my *Animal Speak* book I know that Coyote means Wisdom and Folly. I looked up the definition of Folly on my phone. It means A trait of acting stupidly or rashly. Well, I took the rashly part. :) So I called my friend and asked his advice to make sure I would be safe if I went on my own. He's from the cities. He would know. And plus, Kevin was busy at work and couldn't answer his phone :) So my friend said I would be ok so I went back home and ordered the tickets online, cause it was prepay only, checked Mapquest, wrote down my directions and left for my adventure. Back on the gravel road I saw 2 goldfinches. They made me think that angels would watch over me so as I drove, getting closer and closer to downtown Minneapolis I just kept telling myself not to be scared, that it would all be just fine.

I ended up in the parking lot right across the street from Hell's Kitchen and I didn't even know it! I didn't even see the tour bus right in front of my face till I went to cross the road! LOL The parking attendant was super nice and he had me park right next to the fence under a light. It was THE MOST perfect parking spot one could ask for because here I had been worried about parking in a ramp and getting lost when I came out.

So I went inside and within 15 min 2 women walked in. I smiled and said a hello—like I knew them. That was weird even for me! Molly and Mary both started talking to me and they are kind of from my area so we hung out all night! I wasn't by myself! It was a small venue, smaller than the other bar and I got to stand 1 back from the stage. And when Steven and Michael Thomas, the guitar player, came around and slapped hands, my hand was right in there! I was being outgoing!!! High Five to me!! You all should see Michael play guitar! He puts on quite a show!! He's awesome!!! And Steven Adler plays the drums smiling the whole time! That is the best part because you can SEE how much fun he is having! The whole band is great. Really.

After they finished, Mary said we should check and see if we could get to meet them on the bus. I was leery, you know what happens on the bus ;) But she reminded me of my mom, she was outgoing and a cute little social butterfly and seemed that she had the drive to meet them if she wanted to. Well, it is a good thing I followed them up to the street because the guys were all out on the sidewalk signing autographs and taking pictures with the fans in front of the bus. It was sooooo awesome! I had Steven sign one of his used drumsticks I had gotten for Kevin (Kevin plays the drums too). They must have been out there over an hour it seemed. Being polite and patient the whole time. I was impressed at how cool they were with it all. I've never had the pleasure of meeting rock stars before, any celebrity for that matter and I was shaking like a leaf I was so happy!!!! Molly was laughing at me and she told me that she was having fun just by watching ME be excited! HAHA! I had liked this band so much that I had driven all by myself to see them!! Holy crap!! This was turning out to be the most perfect night!! Afterward Mary and Molly and I hung out listening to another band and then they walked me across the street to my car when it was time to leave. It WAS a perfect night!! I didn't get lost finding my way out of the downtown area either! I drove home so giddy at 3:30am!! I DID IT! I'm not scared to go to the cities on my own anymore AND I made two new friends! I couldn't have asked for a better night.

# UNSELFISH LOVE

"Children are souls that kiss the earth."
—Doris Stokes

I KNOW A LOT OF people are upset with the verdict in the Casey Anthony trial. If they had found her guilty than we would all feel that justice has been served for little Caylee and we would forget about it in a week but maybe by being a Not Guilty verdict we will start taking the steps to make sure that this doesn't happen to more children. We all cannot continue to keep turning our heads and not get involved when we know a child is being mistreated. I believe we all come with a purpose in life and I don't see why it is so hard to think that even a 2 yr old little girl would have a purpose SO GREAT that would save thousands of more children's lives. Our soul makes a decision before we come here and sometimes that decision includes brutal things for the sake of others. I read Angel oracle cards for people and last Tuesday night I shuffled the deck and chose 2 randomly while thinking about little Caylee. These were the two: This Is Your Life's Purpose and Your Children Are Watched Over By Angels. Thank you Caylee for your sacrifice.

# GOD IS PRESENT IN THE CLEAN-UP PROCESS

Not just in the sticks but in each other.

LAST NIGHT WE HAD SOME really strong storms come through our little town with 90 mph winds. Out here at our house we had very little damage but in town there were trees down everywhere like a tornado had went through. Kevin and the kids and I went to his mom's house to help his brother clean up the mess in their yard. I brought the guys that were working across the street some ice water and Kevin went over to the neighbors with his chainsaw to take down their tree that was torn in half. I was thinking how fortunate I am to have a husband that is willing to help people. Then I took this picture of the sticks. There were lots of them making little and big crosses all over the yard. Kevin came into the garage later to get more gas for his chainsaw and was dripping with sweat. He goes, "nice way to spend the day," (kinda sarcastically) and then after a short pause, "Helping people. We should be grateful that we can do that." It made me feel good to be able to experience and see kindness in neighbors helping neighbors all over town today.

# FOLLOW THE SIGNS

GOD NEVER CEASES TO AMAZE me. The day that I decided to publish this into a REAL book, June 24, came as quite a surprise. For the last year I have been going to the bookstore or the library and I would always think, "My book could be in here. It should." but I never really thought I would actually do it! When I woke up that morning last month I had an email from Dr. Wayne Dyer about a free consultation with a publisher. I got out of bed and was going to call it right away . . . totally odd for me because usually I put stuff off. I stopped at my vanity to read my daily reading in the magazine <u>The</u> <u>Upper Room.</u> The reading was from Isaiah 43:20-21 The Lord says, "I give water in the wilderness, rivers in the desert, to give drink to my chosen people, the people whom I formed for myself so that they might declare my praise." Then I saw that I had a new email from the John Edward *Infinite Quest* website that was my daily transit. It said, "it is a great day for desktop publishing work."

I am not even kidding you! THREE things! Hey! Maybe THAT is what Jesus was telling me about 3 that I didn't understand!! Hahaha! I bet it is!! I just thought of that now! That's Great! I love it when He can make me laugh!! Ok. Back to my story. So I called up the number and spoke to a representative, got all the info and told him I would talk to my husband and call him back. From THAT moment on, when I hung up the phone my brain was foggy. I literally went through the rest of the whole day in a fog. Kevin was outside working on the brush pile and the kids were helping him. I told him all about it and he said I should do it if I felt it was right. Man, is he supportive! Then I asked Lexie's opinion because when we get a new hit in another country on my blog we high five. Lexie was excited about it. So I did it. I was nervous but a good nervous. Silently in my head I asked God for a sign. And to be honest, I thought I wouldn't get one because so far all signs pointed to yes BUT one came. We had went out to dinner at a little restaurant on the lake. Kevin had taken the day off and he never had a Friday night off so we were enjoying ourselves. Our friends texted us to ask if we wanted to meet them out for dinner in another town. Kevin texted back no but I said we should go because we never get a chance to hang out with our friends. So we drove over to the other town after we had sat on the deck and enjoyed our food and the view. I had a really good BLT :) Our friends had invited their grandparents because we had said no. When we were all done eating his grandma got up and on her way back to the table she saw out the window a big rainbow so she told the kids to come see. I was up out of my chair immediately. THERE was my sign I had asked for and wasn't expecting. A rainbow that told me not to worry about the book . . . that it would be ok. Good thing we decided to go to meet our friends . . . good thing they had invited their grandparents so the grandma could tell us to look at it . . . see how things happen for a reason? I love that. I love that God will work through others to get a message to you. You just have to have an open mind and an open heart to receive it. It's that easy.

# About the Author

Elizabeth lives in Minnesota with her husband and two children. She likes taking pictures of flowers, walking around her yard, enjoys watching the birds and going to Door County, Wisconsin during the summer months. Her favorite movie is Step Brothers. :)